Edward Reynolds was born in Ghana, West Africa, studied at the University of London, and is now professor of history at the University of California, San Diego, where he specializes in African history. A frequent contributor to scholarly journals, his other books include *Trade and Economic Change on the Gold Coast*.

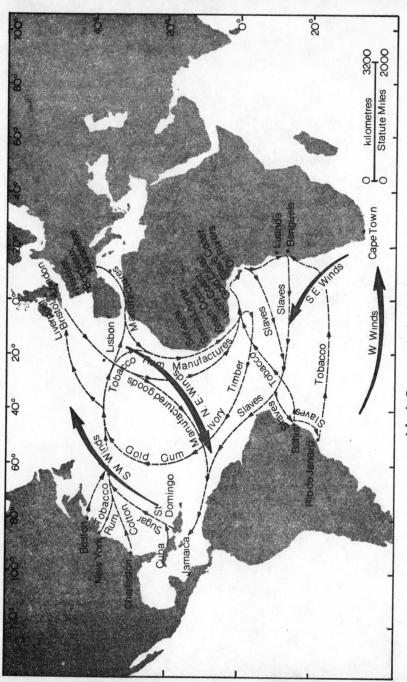

Atlantic Commerce in the Eighteenth Century

STAND THE STORM

A History of the Atlantic Slave Trade

EDWARD REYNOLDS

Elephant Paperbacks
IVAN R. DEE, PUBLISHER, CHICAGO

For
Joel Reynolds

First ELEPHANT PAPERBACK edition published 1993 by Ivan R.
Dee, Inc., 1332 North Halsted Street, Chicago 60622. Manufactured
in the United States of America and printed on acid-free paper.

Library of Congress Cataloging-in-Publication Data:
Reynolds, Edward.
    Stand the storm : a history of the Atlantic slave trade / Edward
Reynolds. — 1st Elephant paperback ed.
        p. cm.
    "Elephant paperbacks."
    Includes bibliographical references and index.
    ISBN 1-56663-020-7
    1. Slave-trade—Africa—History.   I. Title.
HT1322.R45   1993
382'.44'096—dc20   92-43909

Contents

Preface and Acknowledgements

Stand the Storm tries to provide an up-to-date narrative account of Africa and the Atlantic slave trade that synthesizes a large, complex body of scholarship into a concise, readable volume. It is not my purpose to delve into the scholarly debate on slavery and the slave trade but to seek to place the study within the context of developments in the New World that led to the importation of African slaves. What is offered here is an introduction which I hope will encourage students and the general reader to pursue further their interest and to study the excellent and sophisticated monographs that have appeared on slavery and the slave trade in Africa and the Americas. The notes on sources and the bibliography provide guidance for some of the rich literature available on the subject.

Friends and colleagues have offered assistance and encouragement in the preparation of the manuscript. I wish particularly to thank the following for their help: Adu Boahen, Rebecca Bostian, David Eltis, Pieter Emmer, Stanley Engerman, Edith Fischer, Humphrey Fisher, Marie Fleischer, Marion Johnson, Martin Klein, James and Eunice Konold, Patrick Manning, Thomas Metzger, Earl Pomeroy, Mavis Porter, David and Katherine Ringrose, Harry N. Scheiber, Leften Stavrianos and Vincent B. Thompson.

I would also like to extend my deep appreciation to Margaret Busby, my editor for her able help.

John Koramoa provided hospitality in London during research trips. Much of the drudgery of typing the initial drafts and proofreading fell upon Kay Reynolds and I heartily appreciate her assistance and contribution.

This book is dedicated to my son, who has accompanied me on many research trips and has missed much play time for the sake of the story told here.

Stand the Storm

O, stand the storm, it won't be long
We'll anchor bye and bye, O brethren!
Stand the storm, it won't be long,
We'll anchor bye and bye.

(Negro Spiritual)

Introduction

The history of the Atlantic slave trade from Africa belongs as much to the African historical tradition as to the history of the expansion of Europe. There is no doubt that the expansion brought Africa, as well as many other non-European countries, into closer contact with Europe; and while it introduced some of the benefits of Western civilization, such as formal education and technological development, it introduced destructive elements as well.

The pain inflicted by the West on non-Western peoples was probably greatest in the Americas, where the bulk of the indigenous Indian population perished under European exploitation, colonization and diseases introduced into the New World. In Africa, the ravages of the slave trade came as a result of demands for labour to meet plantation needs in the Americas. While it is possible to look at the history of European expansion in terms of its negative impact upon other peoples, it is also necessary to view these non-Western societies as a whole and keep in mind the various dimensions of their relations with the West.

There are three possible interpretations of the effects of Western expansion on traditional societies. First, there is the Marxist view, which dwells upon the wounds inflicted upon the non-Europeans and delineates the disfunctional aspects of imperialism. The Weberian view, on the other hand, sees European expansion as an agent for introducing modernization, and a catalyst for positive growth and change; this view ignores the destructive aspect of European expansion and civilization. A third view, and the one that is followed in this study, looks at Western expansion in terms of the scope of its impact, good or bad. The emphasis here is not only on the baneful effects of the trade but also on the resiliency and resourcefulness of the societies with which Europeans came into contact. The view that I pursue here is, therefore, not one of a passive society being systematically destroyed by a dynamic European society, but of a society that initially met Europe as an equal partner in trade and commerce.

This book differs from previous studies of the Atlantic slave trade in several ways. It uses both primary sources and contemporary scholarly works which reflect recent advances in the study of the slave trade, whereas many older syntheses relied too heavily on books and pamphlets by abolitionists that often exaggerated the slave trade's worst excesses. *Stand the Storm* is not a speculative work; it seeks to avoid ideology and to present a realistic and balanced picture of Africa and the tragedy of the slave trade. It also refutes certain central points of African historiography still current in some quarters: that African slavery was essentially benign, that the Atlantic slave trade completely destroyed African society and that the under-development of Africa began solely as a result of the European slave trade.

The Atlantic slave trade, together with the slave trades of the trans-Sahara and East Africa, was part of a commercial system that brought blacks to many parts of the world.[1] While the trans-Saharan [2] and the East African [3] trade have begun to receive much needed attention, historians have focused primarily on the Atlantic slave trade (see Notes on Sources). Before the emergence of the new historical interest in the slave trade the general conception and presentation of the subject were often confined to the horrors of the slave trade and are filled with moral judgements. That the horrors existed and that the trade was immoral cannot be overstated, but this alone does not broaden our understanding of what is a complex phenomenon.

Recent studies of the slave trade have shifted from the moralistic nature of the earlier works to a more scholarly, analytical examination. Although this is largely a result of a revitalized interest during the last twenty-five years in the study of African history, much of the credit for new directions for research on the slave trade is due to the work of Professor Phillip D. Curtin. His book *The Atlantic Slave Trade: A Census* provides the estimates for analysing global slave imports to the Americas and his work has stimulated research on the quantitative aspects of the trade. Much of this recent research, particularly the works of David Eltis on the nineteenth-century slave trade, and of Paul Lovejoy, have slightly modified Curtin's figures but not his conclusions, and I have relied heavily upon his data.

The investigation of the slave trade has provided rich details for regional studies and contributed to our understanding of local

African economies and their response to foreign trade. The nature of African slavery and its possible relationship to the Atlantic trade have also received serious attention (see Notes on Sources, for chapters 1 and 2 in particular). The new interest in the slave trade is evident in the growing number of conferences and symposia on the subject in recent years.

My purpose is not to write yet another study for the specialists but to provide a short synthesis of the history of the Atlantic slave trade in the context of current research and scholarship. The initial chapter deals with slavery within various African societies. The problems involved in translating African languages are not enough reason for abandoning the term "slavery". While I recognize that slavery is a complex social institution and that its characteristics were not the same in all African societies, I feel that no matter what the variations in African servile institutions, slavery was just that and should be so labelled. The information on traditional African society provides a background for understanding the impact of the slave trade and is presented using various paradigms in order to help the reader gauge the changes that took place during the period of the Atlantic trade. The second chapter deals with slave trading, covering some of the major points such as the organization of the trade by Europeans, and the provenance of slaves for the trade, and the following chapter describes their transportation to the Americas.

In Chapter 4 I examine the factors that led to the demand for slaves in the European colonies in the Americas and how that demand was met. Statistical data is also included to explain the ebb and flow of the imports in people from Africa to the Americas, though I have attempted to keep statistics to a minimum while giving an indication of the violent impact of the trade on the African social world.

The fifth chapter concentrates on the abolition movements in Europe and America. Abolition is presented in the context of the philosophical ideology of the eighteenth century rather than of the humanitarian movement or factors of economic determinism. The discussion includes the efforts of Great Britain to end the slave trade through diplomacy and armed force.

Chapter 6 addresses the impact of the slave trade on Africa, examining the changes and responses of African society in a variety of regions to the European trade, in order to reach conclusions about the impact of the trade on African societies. One may only speculate about what Africa and her economy might have been had the slave trade never existed.

The final chapter deals with the impact of the slave trade on the Americas, placing the trade within the broader context of the commercial relationship between Europe, Africa and the Americas, and within the prevailing mercantilist economic philosophy of the period. The demographic impact of the trade is examined in terms of the survival and distribution of slaves in the Americas, and the cultural impact is measured by the societies and institutions created by people of African descent in the Americas. My emphasis here is on the creativity and innovation of Blacks in the Americas, rather than on the supposition of a linear transfer of African culture and institutions. Finally, I deal with prejudice and white supremacy as a consequence of slavery, and the new consciousness among black people as they seek a new identity in the West.

1
African Slavery and African Society

This is a book about slavery, Africa and Africans. In the polemics about the morality of the Atlantic slave trade, the relationship between black slavery and African society has suffered from generalizations and the lack of a comprehensive perspective. It has been recognized that slavery was common in Africa before the arrival of European slavers, and this has led to a strain of interpretation that points to the readiness of African society to participate in an international system. It has also led to the view of African slavery as an essentially benign institution very distinct from the plantation slavery of the Americas and the Caribbean, thereby deflecting moral judgements on the matter back upon Europeans. These often misleading interpretations require that we begin with a dispassionate overview of slavery in Africa before European influence.

Slavery in Africa

The problems of clearly defining the term "African slavery" have often resulted in a confused understanding of the phenomenon in its various forms. One must go beyond the traditionally held Western view in order to comprehend the institutions that were referred to as slavery in Africa.

In certain African societies what has been called "slavery" may not, in fact, have denoted completely servile conditions but rather a status that could best be translated as that of "subject" or "servant". Among the Asante (Ashanti) of Ghana, for example, the term *akoa* could be translated as slave, subject or servant; different categories existed under the term *akoa* for different degrees of servility. There was *awowa*, which meant a pawn, a pledge, a mortgage or a security for what a person owned. Another term, *odonko*, was applied to a person from the North who had been purchased for the express purpose of enslavement. The term *domum* denoted enslaved war captives, while the appellation *akyere* referred to people living in designated villages who were looked upon as a human reservoir for sacrifices.[1] As these terms suggest, several variables determined the types of servitude in different parts of Africa, including remuneration that the slave received, the degree of coercion involved and the relationship of the "slave" to the normative group in the society, depending on the environment and the needs of the community. Thus it is possible to distinguish between "beneficent slavery", "moderate slavery" and "harsh slavery". The common denominator in all definitions of a slave is that such a person is the property of another politically, is socially at a lower level than the rest of society and performs compulsory labour.[2]

In Africa, as in other parts of the world, warfare was a principal means of recruiting slaves.[3] Prisoners of war were often of little value at the point of capture because they were close to home and were likely to escape; they therefore had to be moved quickly and sold, although the sale of war prisoners did not preclude their captors from keeping some of them for personal use. With the growth of strong centralized states in Africa, warfare for the acquisition of slaves was often turned into a tributary arrangement whereby the weaker states supplied a certain number of slaves to the stronger every year. Raiding and kidnapping were other practices which sometimes terrorized whole areas as men lay in ambush to seize unsuspecting individuals. Strong groups or states raided weaker ones, often forcing the latter either to migrate to other areas or to enter into a tributary or submissive arrangement.

Enslavement was also accomplished through judicial and voluntary processes. Freedom was often forfeited for infraction of certain laws and in compensation for homicide. Hunger drove individuals to place themselves or their children under the protection of others as slaves, particularly during the periods of famine that followed drought or locust plagues. Crimes, quarrels or threats often caused people to flee their own community and place themselves in voluntary slavery. In commercial transactions, war prisoners, kidnapped victims or persons condemned through the judiciary system could be purchased.

The functional use of slaves varied from social to economic, from their employment in plantations or mines and for domestic work to their use as human sacrifices.[4] In areas where servile relationships were present they pre-dated the arrival of Europeans on the African coast.

In 1441, ten Africans from the Guinea Coast had been shipped to Portugal as a curiosity, after a trading expedition, and three years later another expedition brought 235 Africans to the Portuguese port of Lagos. However, long before the Portuguese first landed on the west coast of Africa, slaves were traded for use in the mining industry on the Gold Coast (present-day Ghana), and this practice continued throughout the nineteenth century. From the 1470s until the 1620s the Portuguese played a middleman role, importing slaves to Elmina on the Gold Coast, where by 1482 they had built the castle of São Jorge da Mina, and selling them to African merchants and brokers. The slaves came primarily from Benin, the Slave Rivers, Arguin, the Grain Coast, Kongo and Angola. From 1500 to 1535 alone, 10,000-12,000 slaves were traded.[5] Portuguese slave imports declined after 1540 because of the efforts of the rulers of the Songhai Empire of the Western Sudan to increase the number of slaves they would supply to Dyula merchants, who sold them to work the gold mines of the alluvial forestlands. The need for labour in the mines led the Akan people (Fanti and Asante) of the Gold Coast to acquire slaves in exchange for gold, and other European nations became involved in supplying slaves for this purpose.

During the seventeenth century, English ships were contracted to transport slaves from São Tomé to Elmina, in the 1650s the Dutch imported slaves from the Bight of Benin and Angola, and the Danes traded in slaves from Popo and Ardra in Dahomey.

African traders were also involved in importing slaves for the Gold Coast mines. By 1548, traders from Elmina were buying slaves on the Grain Coast (modern Liberia) and selling them to local dignitaries and gold merchants from the interior. By 1572, traffic in slaves had also developed between the Kwakwa (Ivory) coast and Axim (modern Ghana). The Kwakwa traders carried ivory, textiles and hides to Axim in exchange for slaves, who were probably then taken to the Ankobra River area to work the mines. The trade from the Grain Coast ended early in the seventeenth century, and that between Axim and Kwakwa a few decades later. African Gold Coast merchants also maintained an active trade in slaves with Popo and Ardra through the seventeenth century.

The gold mines and the manner in which slaves were employed there was described by a Portuguese traveller during the sixteenth century:

> The gold mines were seven in number. They are divided among seven kings, each of whom had one. The mines are dug very deeply into the ground. The kings have slaves whom they put in the mines and to whom they gave wives, and the wives they [the slaves] take with them; and they bear and rear children in these mines. The kings, also, furnish them with food and drink.[6]

Slaves who worked these mines for the kings were not the rulers' personal property, but were attached to the state, and they were segregated residentially at the mines. This use of slaves in the mining industry on the Gold Coast continued into the nineteenth century.[7]

As gold mining expanded, there was a need to enlarge the agricultural areas under production to provide food for the miners and, from the fifteenth century onwards, slaves were engaged in clearing the land for cultivation. In the Songhai Empire (1400-1591) slaves worked on royal plantations that were established throughout the empire. The seed for the plantations was provided by the *Askiya*, the ruler of the empire, and the head of each farm had to deliver a yearly quota of grain to him.[8]

In some parts of Africa slaves also functioned as military or administrative officers. In the empire of Mali, slaves and emancipated slaves were among the principal provincial administrators. Frequently the confidants of rulers, these slave officers often intervened in succession disputes and were sometimes known to seize the throne when survival of the empire was threatened.[9]

Slaves historically played an important role as soldiers. Since they lacked kinship ties in the society and were without status outside their relationship with the royals who employed them, they could be trusted with important military responsibilities. In this capacity, they were able to influence the outcome of royal elections in cases where different lineages vied for the same office. Slave warriors in the state of Bambara of the Western Sudan were instrumental in making or breaking candidates for royal office.[10] Slaves employed as royal officers sometimes included eunuchs, castrated male captives who commanded high prices. While most African eunuchs were found in Europe and the Islamic world, some were used in Africa as keepers of harems or as trusted, intimate advisors of royalty.

Slaves were also used for religious purposes. Some Igbo communities in Nigeria had cult slaves known as *Osu*, [11] who either assumed this role voluntarily or took the status by seeking refuge at shrines of local deities in order to avoid being sold into slavery. The status of *Osu* was lifelong. Socially at the bottom of society with no possibility of mobility, the *Osu* were used to exact taxes and consequently were hated by the community. The sacrifice of a slave at the time of the death of a king or important personage served the function of appeasing the spirit of the deceased or providing him with a servant in the world of the spirits. This practice was not devoid of religious significance since African traditional religions involved ancestor worship.

Where slaves were employed in a domestic capacity, they usually fitted into the operations of the household or the kinship group that had recruited them, aiding, supplementing and participating in the normal household labour force. The females might become wives and concubines. They often helped produce and trade textiles and crafts. As well as being used to increase the effectiveness of one's group or for social prestige, domestic slaves represented a form of property and capital acquisition. The nineteenth-century slave trader Theodore Canot realized the economic aspect of African slavery when he wrote:

> The financial genius of Africa, instead of devising bank-notes or the precious metals as a circulating medium, has from time immemorial declared that a human creature — the true representative and embodiment of labour — is the most valuable article on earth. A man, therefore, becomes the standard of prices. A slave is a note of hand that may be discounted or pawned; he is a bill of exchange that carries himself to his destination and pays a debt bodily; he, is a tax that walks corporeally into the chieftain's treasury.[12]

Whatever the function of domestic slavery, it should be stated clearly that its role, use and treatment varied in time and place.

In spite of the indigenous forms of servitude that existed in Africa, the research of the late Guyanese historian Walter Rodney indicates that in areas such as the Upper Guinea Coast there was no slavery until the coming of the Atlantic slave trade. Rodney points out that, during the sixteenth and seventeenth centuries, there were no references to local African slavery from this area. Most of the references to slaves in Sierra Leone during these centuries were rather to political clients, and this kind of clientage was not seen as slavery. Thus, Rodney concludes that the Atlantic trade was responsible for the introduction of slavery into this area.[13] Its prior absence might indicate that this was one of the regions in Africa where labour requirements of the society had not developed to the extent that they required slave labour.

Most slaves, however, were outsiders who had to be incorporated into a new society and into a kinship group.[14] Those in this situation had a relationship of dependency and had to gain access to social relationships. To do this, it was necessary to learn the master's language, be married into the society and propagate. Assimilation depended upon acceptance by members of the host society, and so there were various possibilities. A slave settled in a mining area or on a plantation might become a member of the local society and, with marriage, establish his own kinship group. A domestic slave might become absorbed into the kinship group of his or her owner.

The fact that slaves could be assimilated by the community that enslaved them requires a look at the kinship and lineage systems that constituted cultural bases of African society. It was the kinship group that provided the individual with an identity, purpose and support system, and within this structure the individual lived according to a clearly defined set of protective rights and obligations.

When individuals were acquired as slaves and transferred to another society they became outsiders without identity, social personality or status. Detached from their natural lineage, they entered into a state of limbo that afforded no rights and obligations. Studies by Miers and Kopytoff have described this state of marginality, in which the slave's old social identity had been lost but a new one not yet established.[15] If the outsider was to be retained and utilized, he or she had to be brought into the social structure of the acquiring kin group. The process of bonding to a different society and lineage group would again provide the outsider with a sense of belonging and give that person the subsequent rights, identity and support structure of a new kinship relationship. Thus the newly acquired person and the host community alike worked to reduce marginality and to integrate slaves into the society.

This integration is probably best perceived as a process involving several generations. Slaves could be redeemed by their kinship group or manumitted by their owners, and freed slaves often chose to remain with their former masters. The positions and places of first-generation slaves were markedly different in matrilineal and patrilineal societies. In societies where descent was traced through the mother, children of enslaved fathers and free mothers were regarded as free, since they belonged to their mother's kinship group; the slave who married a free woman and fathered children of free lineage no doubt reduced his own marginality. In patrilineal societies, a slave acquired a wife by virtue of the payment of bride-wealth, and if the slave's owner paid this then any children became the property of the master.

It was possible in patrilineal societies for a slave woman to be given in marriage or in concubinage to a man belonging to another lineage, and children born to the union were considered as slaves. However, it was common for slave women to marry their masters or members of the master's kinship groups, and the children of such a marriage, although their status varied from society to society, were often free.

Among the Igbos of Eastern Nigeria and the Asante of Ghana [16] second-generation descendants of slaves inherited the slave status of their parents. The position of slaves was clear in matrilineal societies like the Imbangala of Angola and the Kongo of Zaïre [17] where children of free women were free, even if their fathers were slaves. In other cases, the children of slave women remained slaves.

In patrilineal societies where material resources were minimal, such as among the Margi of Nigeria, [18] there was little need for differentiation between the descendants of slaves and free men. Those patrilineal societies with greater resources often made differentiations among second-generation descendants of slaves,[19] who became increasingly integrated into the kinship group; slave ancestry was not necessarily a social impediment, nor did it preclude the individual from occupying a variety of roles. In some cases, the everyday life of some slaves and descendants of slaves was indistinguishable from those of free people.

The severity of treatment meted out to those enslaved differed in time and place according to the nature and purpose that they served. The slave's incorporation into the kinship group and the larger structure of the society may be viewed as a form of control over what would otherwise have constituted a large, alien exploited group that might otherwise rebel against and undermine the community.

Notwithstanding the variations of African forms of slavery, it often seemed benign in the picture drawn by the nineteenth-century observers. Brodie Cruickshank, a British merchant on the Gold Coast for eighteen years, depicted African slavery in this way:

> The condition of the slaves in the countries under our protection is by no means one of unmitigated hardship. In ordinary cases, the slave is considered as a member of his master's family, and often succeeds to his property, in default of a natural heir. He eats with him from the same dish, and has an equal share of all his simple enjoyments.[20]

Cruickshank also states that "scarcely a day passes that the English magistrates are not called upon to examine into the validity of a master's right to the person held in slavery by him".[21] These cases were brought to court at the instigation of the slave. If his master could prove legitimate ownership, a slave would have his freedom by paying a redemption price. However, if "the treatment which he has received should appear to have been very bad, he receives a certficate of liberty".[22] British courts had occasion "to grant some thousands" of certificates of freedom to slaves.[23] Of course, had slavery on the Gold Coast been as benign as Cruickshank implied, there would have been no need to free thousands of slaves on the grounds of abuse.

The reluctance of many scholars to accept the *fact of its existence* often creates the impression that cruel and dehumanizing enslavement was a monopoly of the West.[24] Slavery in its extreme forms, including the taking of life, was common to both Africa and the

West. It is not enough to say that slavery in Africa was unlike that of the Western plantations, where it was an exploitative economic as well as social institution. However, the fact that African slavery had different origins and consequences should not lead us to deny what it was — the exploitation and subjugation of human beings. Nevertheless, the whole issue of the forms of slavery in Africa should be placed in the general context of the nature of African society to enable us to assess the impact of the Atlantic slave trade in Africa and comprehend the cultural impact slaves made on the New World society.

The social context of African slavery
Given the size and diversity of the African continent, attempts to describe African societies can often lead to meaningless generalizations or else complex and unwieldy treatments. The daunting task of delineating the features of African societies and cultures can be rendered manageable by looking at their unity and diversity in the following areas: geography, community, occupation, economy and politics.

Physical
The geography of Africa has obviously greatly influenced the continent's history, society and culture. Africa ranks next to Asia in size and covers an area of 11.7 million square miles (30.3 million square kilometres). This huge land-mass is some 3.24 times the size of the United States of America. In spite of its size, Africa has an exceedingly inaccessible coastline with few maritime inlets or large river estuaries. Many of the estuaries that do exist are blocked by offshore bays, shallow depths and rapids. The coastal zones are quite narrow (about 32 kilometres) in width, and coastal swamps have complicated construction of roads and the navigation of rivers.

The northern part of Africa was connected by a narrow bridge to the Near East until 1869 and was, in some respects, part of the Mediterranean world. The Monsoon trade winds of East Africa allowed some contact with people from the Near and Far East who came there to trade. But the area south of the Sahara Desert remained isolated, little affected by the relationship that existed between North Africa and the Mediterranean world. West Africa, which lacks natural harbours, remained largely unknown to the outside world until the Portuguese sailed to the area during the fifteenth century.

Climate influences all human activity in Africa. About 90 per cent of the land can be classified as tropical. The area around the Equator (West Africa and much of the Kongo basin), with high temperatures and humidity, has an equatorial or rain-forest climate. North and south of the Equator, the climate is tropical, becoming drier as the distance from the Equator increases. From this savannah area there is decreasing rainfall and a gradual merging into semi-desert and desert. Beyond the desert zones of the Sahara in the north and Kalahari in the south, the climate is Mediterranean at both ends of the continent. Temperatures in the Mediterranean climate zones are relatively low and these are some of the most favoured parts of Africa. As a whole, however, the major portion of the continent suffers from disabling extremes in climate.

The peoples of Africa are as diverse as its physical contours. Recent research has rejected the classification of Africans into six major groups: Caucasians, Khoisans, Pygmies, Negroes, Erythriotes and Mongoloids.[25] It is no longer tenable simply to link race, language and culture; factors like history, migration, adaptation to ecological environment, genetic exchange and transmission must be taken into account. Genetically, it is impossible for any human group to keep closed or "pure" for an extended period, and inter-mixture makes it difficult to prove common origins in the distant past. Thus genetics, rather than a morphological or phonotypic approach, may be used to explain the diverse groups. The work of linguists supports the view that classification [26] in Africa cannot be made on the basis of race and cultures, since historical factors have changed these relationships. In this context, no correlation can be established between race, language and culture. The more than eight hundred African languages belong to four major groups — Afroasiatic, Sudanic, Congo-Kordofanian and Click — which do not demonstrate any complete relationship between racial and linguistic group classifications. But whatever their language, culture or the nature of the environment, Africans evolved institutions to enable them to live and cope with their ecological surroundings.

Community

Kinship is the key to understanding African society, using the word to refer to descendants of a common ancestor or people who share a physical (sexual) relationship.[27] The family was a basic unit of the kinship structure, within which relatives were often known simply as father, mother, brother, sister. An individual's mother's brother's son or father's brother's son was considered a brother. Kinship was the bond that cemented human relationships in the society and instilled harmony, security, co-operation and a sense of community therein. Since the place of each person in the society was unique, kinship gave everyone identity, meaning, function and purpose. Two basic lineage structures existed in Africa: a patrilineal system and a matrilineal one. In the patrilineal system, descent was traced through the father, who remained the authority figure even when the child became an adult. In the matrilineal system, descent was traced through the mother, and the mother's brother had the ultimate authority over his sister's children. Kinship groups beyond the family were viewed as a lineage; several lineages formed a clan and many clans formed a unitary group or state.

The kinship group was an entity that continued through time and grew and expanded through marriage and childbirth. The manner of acquiring spouses varied greatly in African societies, but marriage often involved the payment of bride-price, a transfer of goods and services which had more symbolic value than economic importance and did not give the man any absolute rights over the woman. While polygamy was common, there also were many monogamous marriages.

Marriage was never considered complete without procreation. Africans believed that without the birth of children the chain of being had been broken, and so they were, and are, highly valued. The names given to children in some African societies underscore this importance. Among the Yoruba of Western Nigeria, names like *Owotomo*, "money is not as valuable as children", *Omodumbi*, "children are sweet to have", *Omololu*, "children are the summit of achievement", and *Omoniyi*, "children are the source of prestige", attested to the value of children.[28] Birth was and is an occasion celebrated by appropriate rites in all African communities. Even before the new-born arrived, preparations were made in anticipation of the event and pregnant women observed certain rites and taboos.

A person normally had to be initiated into the group at an appropriate time, usually at puberty, the ceremony being significant in making that individual a full member of the community. Some societies held initiation rites for both sexes, while other such rites were confined to women.

Among the Mende of Sierra Leone all young people were initiated into adulthood: the men joined the Poro association and the women belonged to the Sande. (The Poro association was also found among people in Liberia and Guinea.) Mende boys were not regarded as mature adults until they had been initiated into the Poro, a ritual which involved being taken to the Poro compound in the bush for several weeks of training and instruction in Mende traditions, customs, the endurance of hardship, self-discipline, co-operation and respect for one's elders. These rites were secret and initiates took an oath of secrecy. The end of the training symbolized the change in status of those taking part and made them full members of the society. Women were similarly initiated into the Sande association.

The system of beliefs and thoughts that ordered the life of each African society included recognition of a supreme God, although African religious systems are often mistakenly generalized in terms such as animism, paganism, fetishism and polytheism. Africans were not animists in the sense of believing that every object had a soul; they did believe that spirits *used* certain objects as their abode and exerted influence through these objects. Paganism is a Western term commonly referring to practices and beliefs of those who were not Jewish, Christian or Muslim, and, as such, is too vague to apply to African religion. A fetish was originally a work of art or object such as a religious charm, but the fact that Africans made use of religious charms should not be allowed to categorize their religious systems. Neither can African religion be adequately described as polytheistic — rather than worshipping many co-ordinate or several gods, Africans recognize a Supreme Being who is above all and is the Creator of any other gods, and is given various names in different areas of the continent. African societies viewed God the Creator as being essentially a life-giving and just spirit, devoid of form. He was everywhere, therefore there were no shrines and temples dedicated especially to Him; there were no feast days set aside for Him or priests appointed to serve Him. The essence of the worship of God was African societies' acknowledgement of His presence and their expression of dependence upon Him.

In addition to their Supreme God, Africans venerated their ancestors. Death, like other rites of passage, was a public affair, when the community was brought together to give the deceased person a proper burial. Many societies believed that the dead entered into a spiritual state of existence, so ancestors were revered, the dead being believed to be able to guard, protect or even punish their descendants. Protection manifested itself through prosperity, fertility and abundant crops. Punishment took the form of epidemics, illness, misfortune and even death. Ancestors who had lived exemplary lives were often singled out for special reverence. Because Africans believed that their ancestors were alive and visited the living, they attempted to keep in touch with them through offerings of food and drink placed on their tombs.

The African pantheon contained other divinities who were created by God to fulfil specific functions, and who could be male or female or good or evil and had abodes in natural phenomena and animals. Some of the divinities were recognized as unique. Of these, the spirit of the earth ranked after God. Since everyone had access to the earth, no temples, shrines or priests were dedicated to it, but sacrifices were made on special occasions, such as the beginning of the planting season. Spirits or deities inhabited bodies of waters of all kinds, and such spirits had priests and shrines and were worshipped and offered sacrifices.

Although all divinities were capable of doing both good and evil, certain deities were considered harmful because they were antagonistic toward people. Among the Yoruba of Western Nigeria, Eshu was known as such a deity, and Sasabonsam was the evil spirit among the Akan of Ghana.

In addition to evil spirits, Africans believed in the mystical forces of witchcraft and magic. Witches were usually women and, occasionally, children who used their powers to harm those they did not like. Belief in witches may have rendered misfortune and adversity more understandable by blaming them on external forces. Magic, also employed to understand the environment, could be used for beneficial purposes. Medicine men used it to attempt healing, and rainmakers used it to encourage rain. Used for anti-social purposes African society called it black magic.

Religion pervaded the lives of all African communities, determining moral and ethical values, and its ultimate function was the establishment and maintenance of harmony, peace and prosperity for the benefit of the society.

Art and music

African art was closely related to religion. Works of art of diverse variety were produced, often related to supernatural forces, faith and the environment. Materials used included wood, metal, stone and clay; although there is evidence of rock painting in the Sahara and in the deserts of South Africa, it was in the area of the plastic arts that we have quantitative and qualitative evidence of the African achievement. African traditional art was expressionist in style and did not represent visual impressions. Sculptured figures were usually symmetrical in form and faced forward, ranging in style from naturalism to the abstract. Art produced in Africa invariably had specific functions. There were art objects that had meaning for the social life of the individual, and could be used in ceremonies concerning birth, initiation or death. For instance, wooden dolls made of wood or glass beads that were ascribed magical powers might be given to girls who were preparing for marriage and procreation.

Such practices appeared among the Dan of the Ivory Coast, the Mossi of Upper Volta and the Chokwe of Angola. In Asante (Ghana), women used a fertility protective doll known as Akuaba ("Akua's child"). Yoruba women in Nigeria frequently carried twin (*ibeji*) dolls in hopes of giving birth to twins, who were believed to bring luck and wealth. If twins were born and one did not survive, the doll was cared for, cleaned and clothed as if it were alive, the belief being that the soul of the dead twin lived in the doll.

Mother-and-child figures were common in the areas of the Kongo and were used as fertility symbols. This preoccupation with fertility explains the prominence of breasts, navels and genitals in African sculpture.

African sculpture frequently depicted ancestral figures in masks that were used on ceremonial occasions. Masks were often carved in secret according to ceremonial tradition, and having been endowed with magic attributes they were supposed to have power and influence over people. They also had other uses and meanings: men who wore masks might belong to a secret society that performed religious functions to honour certain spirits in the name of the community. Among peoples like the Chokwe of Angola, huge masks were worn at the initiation rites when boys were circumcised. Whatever the occasion, the wearer of a mask represented the spirit whose mask was worn. The Dogon of Mali, the Mossi of Upper Volta and the Senufo of Ivory Coast used masks in death rituals to help send the souls of dead people on their journey.

Although there were no personal images to represent God, the Supreme Being, there were portraits to represent the pantheon of gods and ancestors who were revered. The Yoruba called them *orishas*, and there were approximately four hundred of these, each of whom had a different portrayal and characteristic. When the Yorubas celebrated the annual feasts of the figures, the portraits of all *orishas*, duly purified and painted, were carried in procession. Similar religious or supernatural portraits existed elsewhere in Africa.

Sculpture was used in ceremonies of magic designed to invoke supernatural powers through magic. One custom was known as "imitative magic". Rene Wassing has described the manner in which this was accomplished:

> The desired procedure or aim is enacted in ritual. For instance, a model is made of a person who wants to kill; it is pierced with a spike causing the individual to die the same death.[29]

Art was evident in more than religion and magic. It was seen in the manufacture of everyday items like wooden instruments, gourd-bottles used for carrying liquids and beautifully decorated wooden vessels, combs and stools.

Africa developed a wide range of musical resources. Except for the music of North Africa, which derives from the Arab world of the Middle East, much of the music of Africa is distinct from that of the West and the Orient. It is very diverse in expression and function, though cultural interaction has led to borrowing and adaptation.

In many African communities music-making, which was part of social events organized for leisure, was also used in traditional rites and ceremonies and for the performance of community projects. Individual musical expression also existed in all African societies. While music-making in traditional Africa was a voluntary activity, among groups like the Hausa of Nigeria and the Wolof of Senegambia it was correlated to class status; people of low rank performed while those of higher status were content to be entertained.

Musicians in Africa employed a variety of instruments in their performances, though the most common were the idiophones — "instruments made of naturally sonorous materials not needing any additional tension as do strings or drums",[30] and including stick beaters, clappers and rattles. Drums with parchment heads (Membranophones) were also important in Africa and came in a large variety of shapes and forms designed to control tone quality and pitch. Apart from being used to make music, drums also served as signals, for calling or transmitting warnings, or as "speech", when phrases and sentences could be attributed to the rhythms and variations of pitch and tone produced on "talking drums".

Africans also made use of wind instruments (aerophones), which may be divided into three groups: flutes, reed pipes, and horns and trumpets. Flutes made from bamboo or wood, and sometimes from clay, could be used as solo instruments, but were often combined in ensemble with drums. Reed pipes, made from stalks of millet and other plants, were less common than flutes. Trumpets might be made from animal horns and elephant tusks, or bamboo stems and gourds. Like drums, horns and trumpets were used to make music and to convey signals and messages.

String instruments (chordophones) were found in many African societies and were of three basic types: bowed, such as fiddle, harp, lute and zither, plucked, such as the *kora* (harp-lute and harp-zither), or beaten. They were used for personal amusement as well as for outdoor public functions and might be supplemented by hand-clapping, stamping of the feet and songs.

The human voice was important in African music-making, and unusual timbres and nuances of voice were sometimes obtained through stopping the ears, pinching the nose, vibrating the tongue or producing echoes. According to the African musicologist Francis Bebey, "African voices adapt themselves to their musical context — a mellow tone to welcome a new bride; a husky voice to recount an indiscreet adventure; a satirical inflection for a teasing tone, with laughter bubbling up to compensate for the mockery — they may be soft or harsh as circumstances demand".[31]

In an important way, African music evolved from intonations and rhythmic sounds of speech, and, as ministers in some black communities in the United States know, it was easy to move progressively from speech into song. African music tended to focus on percussive sounds that were communicated rhythmically, as was evident in performance techniques and symbolic language. The rhythm so common to all types of African music is not easy to define. But, as Bebey has put it: "Rhythm is an invisible covering that envelops each note or melodic phrase that is destined to speak of the soul or to the soul; it is the reflection of the constant presence of music. It is the element that infuses music with a biological force that brings forth a psychological fruit."[32] However, African music was more than rhythm; it contained a high degree of melodic development and made greater use of polyphony than European music. It was exceedingly important in the life of the African. Again, as Bebey wrote:

> Music is born with each child and accompanies him throughout life. Music helps the child triumph in his first encounter with death — the symbolic death that precedes initiation; it is reborn with the child who is now a man and it directs his steps along the path of law and order that has been laid down by the community.[33]

The dance that African music evoked could be viewed as social and artistic expressions which conveyed feelings on important personal or communal matters through movement, posture and facial expression. Kwabena Nketia has pointed out:

> Music for the dance performs two major functions: it must create the right atmosphere or mood or stimulate and maintain the initial urge for expressive movements; and it must provide the rhythmic basis to be articulated in movement or regulate the scope, quality, speed, and dynamics of movement through its choice of sounds, internal structural changes, or details of design.[34]

Music was related not only to dance but also to events such as the funerals of hunters, priests or chiefs. Religious worship and festivals provided a context for music and drama.

Speech

Speech was closely related to music, much of oral expression in Africa having a melodic quality. Speech and song were, in fact, often integrated. The description of an experience might evolve into song, with a person narrating a tale, or might alternate from speech to song as the unfolding of the story dictated. Listeners might also interrupt with song and speech.

Much of Africa did not have literate communities, and this absence of a literary tradition made proper oral communication even more important. Folktales were handed down from generation to generation, and many societies possessed oral historians who were repositories of the communities' histories. The *griots* of areas such as Senegal and the Gambia are traditionally professional musicians (who may at some time have been slaves) with the duties of preserving and singing the history of a particular family or tribe going back several generations, as well as being required to improvise on current affairs. This reliance on oral rather than on literary skills may well explain the eloquence of African statesmen, as well as the Black clergy in the United States.

The subjects of folktales, which were important in a traditional society, were closely linked to the environment and lives of the people. Folktales served both to instruct and to entertain. They explained origins, chronicled events, extolled courage, honesty, humility and instilled ethics and morality. Commonly appearing in the stories were "trickster" figures — the spider (Ananse, in Ghana), tortoise, rabbit, hare, gazelle and hyena — and the influence of these animal tales extended to the New World, finding echoes in the Uncle Remus stories of the United States and the Anancy stories of the Caribbean.

Stratification and polity

The environment was critical in determining modes of livelihood. Although iron technology was in use in Africa as early as the sixth century B.C. and had extended to practically all parts of Africa by 500 A.D., the plough did not spread through Africa south of the Sahara except for in Ethiopia.[35] Furthermore, south of the Sahara the adoption of the wheel was difficult because of the existence of tsetse flies, which in many areas made survival of draught animals impossible.

Before the arrival of Europeans, most Africans lived in villages or small settlements, although important urban centres did exist. There were important commercial centres in the western and eastern Sudan that linked the area with the commercial centres of Northern Africa. The maritime civilization of eastern Africa had developed important urban centres such as Kilwa and Mombasa, where gold, slaves, ivory and cloves were traded with areas in the Middle and Far East. There were also capital and administrative centres of strong centralized states and these, of course, were involved in trade.

At the time Europe made contact with Africa during the fifteenth century, there were still a few groups, like the Bushmen, who survived as hunters and gatherers. The vast majority of Africans, however, could be classified as farmers and pastoralists. Others combined the two modes of life. Whether they practised farming or herding, they often supplemented their living with hunting.

While most African communities were self-sufficient, they also participated in local, regional and long-distance trade,[36] and the market mechanism that brought this about was the result not just of surplus but also of the process of specialization. Thus, beyond the basic occupations of farming and herding, there were medicine men, priests, weavers and artisans. Division into occupational groups inevitably led to stratification.

In African societies stratification was a function of prestige, power, wealth and age — the last being probably more important in Africa than in any other traditional society. Priests, medicine people, members of craft guilds and others of special skill and members of secret societies also had great prestige. Similar social gradations existed among slaves. Origins, the length of time spent in the community, the generation (first, second or third), the function performed, and opportunity and ability to acquire wealth or movable property all affected the slave's place on the social scale. The division of society into age-sets was a powerful form of stratification, with considerable prestige and respect given to the old. Whatever the position of each person, the various groups and interests ultimately related to the polity of the society.

In order to survive, the government of African societies had to keep order within the social group and protect it from its enemies. The forms of government that operated in Africa may be divided into at least three groups.[37] One type featured a political community that was based on kinship relations. Another type was a society without a centralized political authority, where authority might be vested in a village council, as among the Igbo of Eastern Nigeria. A third type was seen in the states which had kings at the centre with recognized political authority.

As the political communities became larger and more heterogeneous, the complexity of government increased and kinship as a basis for polity became less important. Furthermore, with the increased size of the polity, outsiders, including conquered peoples, became members of the political community. The functions of the polity also grew and were no longer confined primarily to cooperative activities; matters dealt with by the enlarged polity include taxation and law-giving.

With increased complexity came a tendency to specialization. A king or a chief was no longer the only political officer and there developed instead a hierarchy of authorities and public institutions. The polity also became more powerful and privileged. As the anthropologist I. Schapera observed, "From having no command of force at all, it acquires the right and the means to deprive people of property and to inflict corporal punishment or even death; and from being treated with bare respect the chief comes to be a very exalted personage with many unique and outstanding prerogatives."[38] This did not mean that the power of rulers went unchecked and that there were no means, methods and institutions by which subjects could protect themselves.

But whatever the level of development, those in control had to evolve a mechanism for decision-making and authority. The problem of authority was particularly significant when the political community extended control over other groups and newly acquired areas far from the centre. Should a conquered group be allowed to retain its own leaders while recognizing the suzerainty and paying tribute to the conquering society, or should commissioners or rulers from the core be appointed to rule those on the periphery? Associated with the problem of governing the periphery was the creation of new offices to meet new needs.

In Ghana, as the Asante kingdom expanded during the eighteenth century, special officers were created and assigned new responsibilities.[39] The drummers in the palace of the central government were assigned the duty of trading for the kingdom. These traders were given advances in gold dust to trade. Trade and economic activities invariably led to revenue being accrued to the kingdom. A chief (Gyaasewahene) became responsible for the Asante treasury. Other officers included road and communication wardens, police, scouts and sword-bearers. The road wardens were responsible for cleaning the roads in the kingdom and clearing it of any nuisances. The police were stationed permanently along points on roads which crossed into metropolitan Asante and collected tolls and taxes. The presence of these sword-bearers guaranteed the official character of the missions.

To maintain authority, states need coercive units like the military and courts to maintain and uphold their decisions.[40] Almost all African societies had some form of military organization. Sometimes the army consisted of age-grades or bands of local soldiers who fought together. In other states, the army was made up of amalgamated troops. Among the Asante, each chief had his own force but was obligated to join the Asantehene (king) in his warfare. Recruiting for the Asante army was often done through quotas imposed on conquered chiefs, and normally a contingent from recently conquered peoples formed the vanguard of the next campaign. Slaves were also used as soldiers, as was the mass transfer of conquered populations.

Most African societies had laws and regulations, and forms of behaviour which were against societal norms often resulted in reprimand, reprobation, punishment, exclusion or death.[41] Included among anti-social acts were sacrilege, incest, witchcraft, evil magic, theft and murder. The society invoked sanctions against deviant behaviour: there were moral sanctions whereby the community showed disapproval, and supernatural sanctions whereby the guilty individual was threatened with misfortune such as sickness or death. When supernatural sanctions were broken, ritual acts of expiation or purification had to be performed to prevent divine retribution. When an individual was accidentally killed or murdered, relatives or members of the victim's kinship group were obligated to retaliate, but in a regulated act of vengeance that was designed and limited to satisfaction.

As in most societies, wars of conquest were prevalent in African history, many groups being dispersed and regrouped as a result. Inter-group feuds, though indistinguishable from war by earlier non-African writers and historians, constantly occurred. When force was used, it was the decision of those at the head of the polity.

The head of the polity was involved also in cultural aspects: maintaining values, sustaining educational functions for the socialization of the young and religious and social ceremonies which were necessary for the recreational and spiritual well-being of the society. In addition, the economic function of the polity was vital to the health of the state: the receipt and regulation of tribute played an enormous role in maintaining services and institutions. More organized and complex polities maintained courts and capitals that utilized agricultural workers, cooks, ritual specialists, keepers of state regalia, military guards, consorts and traders; but although participation in economic activity and production supplied some of the resources needed to maintain polities, tributes, as stated, formed an important source of wealth.

African polity, like other aspects, can be oversimplified and made to appear static. However, this general discussion of the continent's cultures is not intended to provide an unchanging view of society but rather to provide a baseline for an understanding of traditional society, its interaction with outsiders during the period of the slave trade, and the transfer of African cultures overseas.

As would become evident in the days of the slave trade, the hedonistic needs of certain rulers overshadowed public need. Trade items like liquor and silks were sought after for the pleasure of certain individuals rather than for the good of the whole. Furthermore, public goals were often sacrificed for the rewards of personal power. The triumph of personal authority often went hand in hand with economic and political power for African leaders, and purely economic motives would not always be easy to discern when Europeans started to trade with Africans by sea from the fifteenth century onwards. Before analysing the demand, conditions and circumstances that led to the ebb and flow of slaves from Africa to Europe and European colonies, however, we should look at the structure of the kind of slave trading which involved the partnership of Africans and Europeans.

2
The Slave Trade

The magnet that initially drew Europeans to Africa was gold, rather than slaves. On what was known as the Gold Coast the trade in the metal began with the Portuguese in the fifteenth century and later attracted the English and the Dutch.[1] The Dutch, who ousted the Portuguese from the Gold Coast between 1637 and 1642, sought to confine their commerce to gold; when they began trading slaves in other parts of the African coast, they refrained from doing so on the Gold Coast, feeling that wars and slave-trading activities were not conducive to gold mining and trading.[2] The English did not officially start dealing in slaves until 1663, when Parliament granted the Company of Royal Adventurers of England Trading to Africa the monopoly for the slave trade on the African coast. Some forty-three years earlier, an Englishman, Richard Jobson, had refused to purchase or deal in slaves, probably because English colonies had no need for them at the time. In his words, "we were a people who did not deale in any such commodities, neither did we buy or sell one another, or any that had our own shapes".[3]

In spite of the importance of gold and other items, with European expansion the direct sea export of Africans abroad increased to meet the plantation and mining needs of the New World. The outposts of European power in Africa were the coastal trading forts and castles which served as warehouses of the slave trade. African chiefs and the principal men of African societies joined the Europeans to establish a trade relationship that facilitated the export of slaves from Africa.

Although the demand for slaves was external to Africa, there were African factors that favoured the rapid growth and maintenance of the trade. Foremost among them was the geographical position of Africa, convenient for transport of slaves to America. In addition, many African societies were small, disunited and poorly armed, unable to defend themselves against slave-raiders or those who conquered them and demanded tribute in the form of slaves. In practice, African societies rarely sold their own people or those who were culturally close to them. Rather, they sold foreigners obtained from distant areas through trading networks and markets. Just as Europeans rationalized slavery by saying that the slave trade would only have been immoral were the Africans human beings with souls like themselves, so too did Africans rationalize that the victims of the trade were "only" foreigners or "trouble-makers".

The slave trade was difficult to stop once it got under way. In the 1630s and 1640s, Queen Nzinga Nbande of Matamba in Angola unsuccessfully tried to co-ordinate resistance to Portuguese slave-traders. Hostility from the Portuguese and neighbouring African slave-trading states pressured the queen to resume trade with them. A century later, in what is now the Republic of Guinea, Tomba, the leader of the Baga, tried to stop the trade but encountered opposition from resident Europeans, mulattos and Africans who were involved in it.[4] Agaja Trudo, one of the greatest kings of Dahomey, had very little sympathy for the slave trade. One of his apparent motives for invading the coastal Aja kingdoms was to restrict and eventually stop the trading in slaves and replace it with legitimate commerce.[5] Agaja issued an invitation to Europeans:

> If any tailor, carpenter, smith or any sort of white man that is free be willing to come here, he will find very good encouragement and be much caressed and get money if he can be contented with this life for a time.[6]

Preparation for the acquisition of Africans for export began in Europe, where capital, ships, crews and goods for trading in Africa had to be secured. Since slave trading involved heavy risk, merchants frequently formed partnerships in order to reduce their losses in the event of unsuccessful ventures.[7] In France, family partnerships were important and geographical factors were considered in forming short-term associations for the conduct of the trade. If no one in the partnership owned a ship, one was purchased. The final step was securing a captain with a reasonable amount of experience, who would have the skill required to deal for slaves with chiefs and merchants on the African coast.

The ship captains who led thousands of slave-trading voyages to Africa were a varied lot.[8] Two about whom we know a good deal from their memoirs are John Newton and Hugh Crow. Newton was born in London in 1725 and died in 1807, the year in which the slave trade was abolished. He lost his mother when he was seven, and his father, who was a master of ships in the Mediterranean trade, sent him to boarding school. At the age of ten, Newton left school and went to sea. After experiences as a sailor and as a resident slave-trader on the coast of Sierra Leone, he became captain of a slave vessel, the *Duke of Argyle*, in 1750. He made four voyages to the African coast before giving up the trade for the Anglican priesthood. (He was later to write many popular hymns, among which were "Amazing Grace" and "How Sweet the Name of Jesus Sounds".)

Hugh Crow, who came to be identified as a one-eyed captain, having lost his right eye in an accident at the age of twelve, was born in Ramsay, Isle of Man, in 1765. His upbringing in a sea-port town gave him the desire for life at sea and he made his first voyage in 1782. He was a pugnacious man, always involved in fights and disputes during his years as a mariner. He had the dubious honour of being master of the *Kitty Hawk Amelia*, the last vessel to sail legally from Liverpool to Africa, on 27 July 1807, with the purpose of carrying slaves to the West Indies.

Besides captains, officers and experienced sailors had to be recruited for the voyage. Surgeons were employed, especially during the eighteenth century, and carpenters, sail-makers and coopers were also essential. The rest of the crew often consisted of novices and young people who were running away to sea. To this assortment were added those who were tricked into becoming sailors on slave boats. As to their quality, Captain Newton stated:

> We are for the most part supplied with the refuse and dregs of the nation. The prisons and glass houses furnish us with large quotas of boys impatient of their parent or masters, or already ruined by some untimely vice and for the most part devoid of all good principles.[9]

Other sailors were procured by fraudulent means from "crimps" and landlords. Crimps lured the unwary into debt and then had them put in jail, with no chance of escape or release except for duty on a slaver. The crimps sometimes "reserved" people in jail for slavers. By the eighteenth century, crimps were being paid £3-4 per trip per sailor.

Seamen were generally treated fairly well during the beginning of a voyage and were given adequate rations. Once they were out to sea with little chance of deserting, their fare deteriorated. Food rations were shortened, and water allowance was reduced to a minimum, and in general their needs received scant consideration. According to Newton:

> There is no trade in which seamen were treated with so little humanity. . . I have myself seen them when sick, beaten for being lazy till they had died under the blows.[10]

The scheduling of arrival on the African coast was extremely important. The rainy season greatly affected the health of Europeans as well as the movement and trading of slaves. As John Barbot wrote:

> the prospeerest [sic] season to render the Guinea voyages most prosperous and safe, is to depart from Europe about the latter end of September, to enjoy the good season on the coast and to have sufficient time to carry on the trade there, so as to reach the Leeward Islands of America by the latter end of April following, which is the time they make sugar there; so that ships may have their full loading, and sail thence for Europe again before the boisterous weather, which usually reigns on our coasts from the beginning of October.[11]

Most British vessels cleared port during the third quarter of the year, especially during July and August. In France, most slave ships left for the African coast in May, June and July with about 60 per cent of the slavers clearing port between 1 May and 31 October.[12] The time of departure had to be calculated according to the distances to various African destinations. Vessels left Europe with precise instructions as to where to proceed on the African coast, which contacts to make in Africa and where in the New World to sell their "cargo". The slave ships were loaded with assorted goods such as beads, textiles, guns, gunpowder, copperware, cowries, amber, Jamaican rum and Virginia tobacco. These goods were selected carefully to meet the demands of the intended place of trade, for failure to cater to African needs and tastes could cause lengthy delays and endanger a successful voyage.[13]

The slave markets that European ships frequented were located in the region between Senegal and Angola in South-West Africa.

The major slave-trading regions, from the fifteenth to the nineteenth centuries, were Senegambia, Upper Guinea (which comprised the area south of Gambia, including the modern states of Guinea-Bissau and Sierra Leone), the Windward Coast (the Cape Mount to the borders of the Gold Coast), the Gold Coast, the Bight of Benin, the Bight of Biafra, the Kongo and Angola.

The Senegambia area was one of the first major sub-Saharan regions to export slaves by sea to Europe and the New World.[14] The Upper Guinea coast was important during the period when the Portuguese were leading slave-traders, and about one-third of the slaves exported overseas during the sixteenth century came from there. The zenith of slave trading from this area was reached in the middle of the eighteenth century, when fighting related to Islamic *jihads* (holy wars) generated slaves for export. The Upper Guinea coast was also one of the early suppliers of slaves in the fifteenth and sixteenth centuries. The tempo of slave trading on the Windward Coast was slow during most of the period of the Atlantic slave trade and the supply of slaves from there was small and irregular. Because this coast lacked natural harbours and good landing places, no European traders resided there to conduct commerce. By contrast, the Gold Coast, a primary slave centre, had about twenty-five major forts and castles and an equal number of small trading factories. Among these European footholds in Africa were those at Axim, Elmina, Cape Coast, Shama, Anomabu, Commenda, Dixcove, Cormantine and Christiansborg.

The Bight of Benin, also known as the Slave Coast, became a major supplier of slaves during the eighteenth century. In the Bight of Biafra, slave trading became important in the late seventeenth century, and by the end of the eighteenth century the area was the leading slaving zone in Africa. The Kongo also became one of the early important regions for the slave trade, but the major part of the trade gradually shifted southwards to Angola after the middle of the sixteenth century.

The Portuguese dominated slave trading on the African coast until the beginning of the seventeenth century, when the main features of the trade became fixed, and at first they secured captives through banditry and kidnapping.[15] Many Portuguese, including Antam Gonçalves, commander of the expedition that can be said to have inaugurated the Atlantic slave trade in 1441 by bringing the first Africans to Portugal for Prince Henry the Navigator, and the pioneer slave-trader Nunez Tristan, lost their lives in attempts to capture Africans; and so great were the outrages committed in the efforts to secure slaves that Prince Henry, who sponsored the Portuguese voyages of exploration, issued orders to prevent such excesses. By 1456 piracy and kidnapping had given way to exchanges between Africans and Europeans, and although an occasional ship's captain still conducted raids, a regular trade with basic patterns for its conduct was established.

Sources of the slaves

Initially, the African sea coast furnished a large number of the slaves sold to the Europeans; but, with increasing demand, Africans were obliged to resort to the back country. Whether they came from the interior or the coastal area, however, slaves were mainly acquired through warfare, kidnapping, tribute and enslavement through the judicial system. A study of 179 liberated slave informants supplied by S.W. Koelle in his "Polyglotta Africa" shows that 34 per cent were war captives, 30 per cent were kidnapped, 7 per cent were sold by relatives or superiors, 7 per cent were sold because of debts, 11 per cent were condemned to slavery through the judicial process and the other 11 per cent were enslaved for unspecified reasons.[16] Since these are nineteenth-century statistics, we cannot assume that the earlier sources of the trade followed this pattern.

Wars produced slaves for the Atlantic slave trade as they had for the supply of domestic slaves. At times, however, what were termed wars were in reality raids. Although wars motivated by economics were difficult to differentiate from those fought for political purposes, many contemporary writers asserted that African wars were fought solely to secure slaves for sale. Describing slaves obtained through warfare in the Senegambia, Barbot writes that "Those sold by the blacks are for the most part prisoners of war, taken either in flight, or pursuit, or in the incursions they make into their enemies territories".[17] John Matthews, who traded in Sierra Leone, also states: "The best information I have been able to collect is that great numbers are prisoners taken in war and are brought down, fifty or a hundred together, by the black slave merchant."[18] Further evidence of slaves as prime military booty is to be found in the journal kept by a surgeon from Liverpool in 1724; his entries of 29 and 30 December, respectively, record:

> No trade today, though many traders came on board; They informed us, that the people are gone to war within [sic] land, and will bring prisoners enough in two or three days; in hopes of which we stay.
>
> No trade yet, but our traders came on board to-day and informed us the people had burnt four towns of their enemies, so that tomorrow we expect slaves.[19]

A former slave-trader, the Reverend John Newton, also supported the view that wars were fought mainly to secure slaves:

> I verily believe, that the far greater part of the wars, in Africa, would cease, if the Europeans would cease to tempt them, by offering goods for slaves. And though they do not bring legion into the field, their ways are bloody. I believe, the captives reserved for sale are fewer than the slain.
>
> I have not sufficient data to warrant calculation, but I suppose, not less than one hundred thousand slaves are exported, annually, from all parts of Africa, and that more than one-half of these are exported in English bottoms.[20]

The issue of the extent to which economic incentives or political motives affected the procurement of slaves has intrigued historians.[21] To assert that wars were fought exclusively for economic gain, however, is to distort reality. Political and economic motives may not be easily distinguishable. While causes for war, resulting in the acquisition of slaves, differed from area to area, the decision to instigate war was made by the polity. The question, then, is what motivated a polity to sanction war? A leader might declare war for economic, strategic, ideological or religious reasons. Economic motivation for war might involve the desire to control trade routes, resources, territory or booty, which in the present discussion will include slaves. Strategically war might be declared to maintain the balance of power or to prevent rebellions and insurrection, or ideological reasons might explain a military decision. Such values, however, might be underlined by economic interests. The conquest of another tribe and the acquisition of territory could bring economic benefits, but a polity might ideologically justify its action in terms of the balance of power, the prestige of its leaders and the solidarity of the group. Religious motivations, as in the Islamic holy wars, often influenced the decision for battle. Whatever the reasons and motivation for war, it was possible to derive economic advantages.

Following war, further slaves could be procured through annual tributary arrangements. Asante in the Gold Coast, for example, secured large numbers of slaves from the areas that she conquered during the eighteenth century. Although it is difficult to quantify tribute as a source for the slave trade, along with wars and raids it provided an important resource.

Kidnapping [22] produced slaves for the Atlantic slave trade, and individuals found alone in isolated places were often victims. The eighteenth-century slave-ship surgeon Alexander Falconbridge was convinced that kidnapping and crimes were the chief support of the trade. In any case, enough people were enslaved by this method to cause apprehension among populations. The fear of being kidnapped often led to Africans travelling in large armed groups. According to Barbot, an "Abundance of little blacks of both sexes were stolen away by their neighbours, when found on roads in the woods".[23] One kidnap victim was Olaudah Equiano, also known as Gustavus Vassa, who came from the coast of modern Nigeria, and it is illuminating to read his personal experience. Prior to his own capture Vassa had seen, from the top of a tree in his yard, people attempting to kidnap children from the home of his neighbour. From his vantage point he raised an alarm and the culprit was arrested. Before long, Vassa and his sister were seized while alone and taken into the forest for eventual sale on the coast.[24]

Economic motives for kidnapping were clear. William Bosman, the Dutch factor on the West Coast, noted:

> The inhabitants of Coto do much mischief, in stealing those slaves they sell to the Europeans, from the upland country — that the inhabitants of Popo excel the former; being endowed with a much larger share of courage, they rob more successfully, by which means they increase their riches and trade.[25]

A practice closely related to kidnapping was "panyarring", or the forcible seizure of a person subsequently sold into slavery, which could be classified as an extra-judicial process whereby a creditor seized a person for debt, for revenge or to assuage personal honour.

Individuals were also condemned to slavery for alleged crimes, and, by the seventeenth century, the laws of societies such as Upper Guinea functioned as a handmaiden to the trade. A traveller reported that "The Kings are so absolute, that upon any slight pretence of offence committed by their subjects, they order them to be sold for slaves without regard to rank, or profession".[26] In the area of present-day Ghana, according to Anthony Benezet, "Some of the negroe rulers, corrupted by the Europeans, violently infringe the law of Guinea".[27]

Adultery and the removal of fetishes were two infractions that led to slavery. Among groups like the Tio, Ngunguly and the people of Iboke in modern Zaïre, slavery was often the punishment for convicted adulterers who were unable to pay a fine, which was equal to the value of a slave when sold. The Akwamu kings and chiefs of the Gold Coast often took women who were married to them in name only. At the end of the year, the women were asked to identify men who had slept with them, and these men were then sold into slavery if not redeemed by relatives. Also on the Gold Coast, fetishes, consisting of pieces of wood, old pitchers or kettles, were often laid in pathways, and those displacing them were seized and sold or had the price of a slave exacted from them.[28]

By the end of the sixteenth century, "those who administered poison to or placed a fetish on others, adulterers with the king's wife, and those who solicited war against the king or asked the Xinas to bring about his death"[29] could legally be made slaves in the Upper Guinea coast. In addition, indebtedness and offences against taboos were cause for slavery. The "law of the land" provided ample scope for fraud, especially in cases involving adultery and witchcraft. In some instances, whole families had to follow the convicted individual into slavery as though they themselves had committed sins for which all their descendants must suffer.

Recent research on south-eastern Nigeria indicates that accused individuals sold through the judicial system were the mainstay of the slave trade in that area.[30] Thieves, poisoners, witches and adulterers were among those victimized. The Igbos of Nigeria believed that the birth of twins was unnatural; thus, mothers of twins, allegedly having allowed evil spirits to enter their wombs, were sold into slavery. In former times, they would have been put to death or banished. According to the historian David Northrup:

> The Igbo recognized a wider range of abominations (*nso*), such as a child whose upper teeth appeared before its lower, who walked or talked sooner than was usual, who had supernumerary fingers or toes, or who had any other deformity, or a woman who menstruated before attaining the "proper" age, gave birth to twins, or climbed trees. Depending on the circumstances, such a person might be killed outright, ritually cleansed, or sold into slavery.[31]

Thus, in many areas crimes that would have evoked the death penalty or compensation now resulted in enslavement.

The trade in slaves stimulated a demand for goods that were novel to the area. It was not uncommon for people to sell their children to gratify new desires, or offspring might be sold to relieve debts or financial difficulties. Among the Tio of Zaïre, a maternal uncle could approach his niece's or nephew's father for money and if the father could not help, he asked to sell one of his children. Parents sometimes sold children whom they were unable to feed during periods of great famine. In times of very serious famine large numbers of families in the area of Zaïre offered children for sale at the same time, which led to the depressing prices and little profit for the sale of young people. Slaves who had been sold by their people were unlikely to escape, since they had no place to go.

The delivery system of the slave trade within Africa was generally characterized by monopolistic restrictions.[32] In the savannah area from the Senegambia basin to Lake Chad, as in other areas beyond the forest region, the trade was controlled by Muslims who, with their agents, formed trading caravans that at times involved up to 1,000 people. The caravans were bought and sold *en route*, and, because of the capital involved in such an enterprise, small traders were often eliminated.

From the Bight of Benin to the Gold Coast, strong states like Akwamu and Oyo in the seventeenth century and Oyo, Dahomey and Asante during the eighteenth century controlled the procurement and sale of slaves. The ruler of Oyo and his court prevented merchants in the area north of them from passing through their territory and allowed royal traders unrestricted access to the trade. Although slave trading in Dahomey was not a complete monopoly, the state had a strong commitment to official control of slaves and severely restricted the internal movements of European traders on the Dahomey coast.[33] Asante also maintained monopolistic practices over the slave trade and employed state traders. After their conquest of the coast, the Asante collected ground rent from the Europeans who maintained forts there.

The same monopolistic practices extended from the area of the Benue River to the Bight of Biafra. During the period when the Bight of Biafra was the largest exporter of slaves for the Atlantic trade, the Ekpe society of Calabar, the marketing and trading networks of the Aro and merchants from Ijaw, Aboh, Igala, Awka and Oguta dominated the trade.

The Ekpe was a secret society that regulated and maintained order in commercial activities at Calabar and imposed sanctions against those who violated trade regulations:

> First it could boycott a person, by having Ekpe blown against him, which would prohibit anyone from trading or having any other dealings with the offender. Secondly, it could place a mark on someone's property which prevented its being used until the mark had been removed. Thirdly, it had the power to impose fines. Fourthly, it could arrest an offender and detain him or hand him over to the person with whom he was at odds. Fifthly, it could execute an offender, either by decapitation, or by tying him to a tree in the bush with his lower jaw removed. Sixthly, it could confine people to their quarter by hoisting a yellow flag. And lastly, it could destroy a man's property.[34]

The Aro trading organization, with the establishment of extensive commercial networks in the interior of south-eastern Nigeria dating from the seventeenth century, has intrigued historians of the slave trade.[35] The Aro originally came from the town of Arochuku, and their settlements, large and small, penetrated the south-eastern Nigerian area. Their trade dominance has been attributed to their exploitation of the "Oracle Arochuku", who demanded from litigants human sacrifices who were eventually sold into the overseas trade. The military dominance of the Aro, who controlled arms in the interior because of their monopoly of European goods, and their skill in maintaining good trade relationships with neighbouring communities and with suppliers, have also been noted.

Whereas the Arochuku Oracle was powerful in the hinterland of south-eastern Nigeria, it was not employed to promote trade in areas where Aro did little or no business. Because of the reputation of the Oracle, many people in the hinterland were fearful of harming "Child of Chuku", or "God-man", as the Aro were called. However, it is not likely, as was once believed, that the Oracle served as a conduit for a large number of the slaves exported from south-eastern Nigeria. Furthermore, military strength was not the decisive element in Aro success, even though their ready market for slaves might have provoked raids on the part of other tribes. The Aro were not politically organized although, given their success in trade and commerce, they could have attempted to create a territorial empire.

While the Aro were heavily involved in the integration, supply and wholesale aspects of the delivery system, agreements and co-operation with various groups and neighbouring communities facilitated the movement of slaves. Although the Aro were by far one of the most successful slave-trading groups, there were similar groups in south-eastern Nigeria that blocked Aro expansion and maintained their own trading networks.

A different delivery system operated in the Angolan area during the first part of the seventeenth century.[36] Agents were sent to buy slaves in the interior on the borders of Kongo and Angola. Among the most important markets were the fairs of the Mpumbu near Stanley Pool. The agents were called *pumbeiros*, or *pombeiros* (from the native word that means "hawker"), and were mulatto sons or trustworthy slaves of the Portuguese. In some instances, the *pombeiros* did not return to Luanda, the capital of Angola, for years but stayed in the interior and periodically received merchandise from the coast, which they exchanged for slaves. Portuguese governors obtained slaves from tribal chiefs and through conducting raids. Slaves were also brought from the Angolan interior by merchants who accompanied Portuguese soldiers during the wars of Portuguese conquest and bought war captives from the troops.

Whatever the mechanism for the procurement of slaves, they

were always brought to the coast for sale. Many first went through various markets and masters, some being used as domestics or as field hands during the planting or harvesting season, before being brought to the coast. Slaves coming from the interior were chained together to prevent their escape. According to Francis Moore, an English factor on the River Gambia, "their way of bringing them is tying them by the neck with leather thongs, at about a yard distant from each other, thirty or forty in a string, having generally a bundle of corn or elephants' teeth upon each of their heads".[37]

European trade for slaves on the African coast basically took two forms: ship trade and factory trade. Slavers without agents on the coast often resorted to sailing from area to area, collecting a few slaves at a time until they had a full cargo. Agents employed by European monopolies often secured slaves from African traders in readiness for the arrival of ships. In order to expedite the delivery of slaves, some agents gave goods on credit to Africans to use for trade in the interior. John Barbot described this practice at Whydah:

> If there happens to be no stock of slaves there, the factor must trust the blacks with his goods, to the value of one hundred and fifty, or two hundred pounds; which goods they carry up into the inland country, to buy slaves at all markets, for about six hundred miles up the country, where they are kept like cattle in Europe.[38]

Resident European agents or factors were successfully used, men who had gone to the African coast hoping to make their fortune, though many perished in the fever-ridden climate of the African coast. One of the more corrupt traders was a man referred to simply as Mr Ormond:

> He left England in 1764, a cabin-boy in a slave ship, and became assistant in a slave factory on the Sierra Leone river. He was industrious and ambitious, and after a few years set up a factory of his own north of Sierra Leone. Illiterate, he grew, nevertheless, a rich and expert slave trader. His cruelty was a byword on the coast. He rid himself of his unsaleable slaves by fastening stones to their necks and drowning them in the river during the night. One Christmas day an English clerk incurred his displeasure. In drunken fury he ordered his slaves to tie up the European, and gave him four hundred lashes. The white man died a few days later.
>
> It was reported that when Mr Ormond caught one of his black wives

having an affair with one of his slaves, he tied her to a tar barrel and set her on fire.[39]

There were others like the Irishman "Nick" Owen, who started trading in slaves in the region of Sierra Leone in 1754 in an effort to recoup a lost family fortune: "If any of the blacks come, I buy their commodities at as cheap a rate as I can, which enables me to trade aboard the ships once or twice a month, which just keeps me from sinking in the principle stock."[40]

Afro-Europeans, the mulatto offspring of sexual encounters between African women and European traders, filled a vital middleman role. In places such as the area between Senegal and Sierra Leone they clung to the traditions of their mothers and kept a distinct form of tribal life. In areas like the Gold Coast, where many mulattos grew up in the coastal towns attached to the various fortresses, they were removed from tribal life and were not subject to the traditional local jurisdiction. They often became interpreters and advisors to chieftains and resident European traders, and some attained positions as successful brokers and merchants.

One of the more prominent mulattos was a man identified as Henry Tucker. According to John Newton, this was "the man with whom I had the largest connexion in Business and by whom I was never deceived".[41] Nick Owen describes him as

> a man who had acquired a great fortune by his skill and some other abilities in the way of trade. . . . He has been in England, Spain and Portugal and is master of the English tongue; he has six or seven wives and numerous offspring of sons and daughters; his strength consists of his own slaves and their children, who have built a town about him and serve as his *gremetos* [retainer] upon all occasions. This man bears the character of a fair trader among the Europeans, but to the contrary among the blacks. His riches set him above the Kings and his numerous people above being surprised by war; almost all the blacks owe him money, which brings a dread of being stepped upon that account, so that he is esteemed and feared by all who have the misfortune to be in his power. . . .[42]

During the era of the slave trade, Portuguese became the commercial language for the coast and remained so even when Portugal was no longer the dominant European nation on the African coast. Some Portuguese terms which became part of the trade language were: *caboceer* (chief or head man), *dash* (gift or bribe), *bozal* (slave shipped directly from Africa), *panyar* (kidnap), and *barracoon* (a shelter where slaves were stored).

Trading for slaves

European ship captains and slavers who came to the African coast were required to acquire a licence to trade by paying stipulated fees or by purchasing a number of slaves at a specified price from the local chief before commencing their regular trade. Regardless of the form, some kind of permission was often necessary for "breaking trade", as this procedure was sometimes called. The dues and numerous presents given by slave traders to Africans in order to do business were complicated and subject to change at the behest of the local people. Customs and dues were generally payable on all exports and imports; the Europeans made every effort to comply with this system of "dashes" (gifts) and dues in order not to do anything that would jeopardize their trade. A slave-ship captain who visited the Gambia River described the process:

> When a ship arrives in the River Gambia she comes to an anchor at Gillofree Port; in the Kingdom of Barra, opposite James Fort on James' Island. . . . You send your boat on shore to acquaint the Alkaide or Mayor of the town of your arrival; he in common returns with the boat, and receives your anchorage-money. Ten gallons of liquor for the king, value 30s, and two iron bars for himself, value 7s, and perhaps presents, a few bottles of wine, beer, cider, etc. He immediately dispatches messengers with the liquor as above to the king, informing him that such a vessel is arrived, and only wants to pay his Customs, intending to proceed up river. The king consults his councillors for a proper day to receive the same; and sends word to the Alkaide accordingly. After a detention of four, five, six and seven days, he sends his people to receive his Custom, 140 bars in merchandise, amount sterling on the average £16.[43]

Similar practices were evident all over the African coast, and by the late eighteenth century "customs" cost close to £400 per ship.[44]

In Whydah, Dahomey, the custom and dues of the king were fixed at twenty-five slaves for every ship that called at the port. Once the ruler was paid, shots were fired to open trade. Traders in Whydah bore the additional cost of securing canoes and the necessary labour to carry their goods from the ship to mud-walled forts three miles inland.[45] Traders had no redress if the carriers stole some of their goods. In Ardra in Dahomey the King's custom was fixed at fifty slaves, and six additional slaves were paid to his son for the cost of wood and water. These charges were not reduced when the King of Dahomey conquered the coast. Barbot stated:

> The duties which the Senegal Company pays to the Black Kings, and fees to their officers, are of two sorts, inward and outward. The inward duties at Senegal river amount to 10 per cent of goods in season or out of season, as they call them. Those for exportation are reckoned thus, one bar of iron for a slave . . . besides some petty fees to the Alkaides, Gerafos, captains of wood and water, which amount to three per cent and are troublesome enough to discharge, being paid at several times and places, and in sundry sort of goods.[46]

In some areas, slaves were purchased with what passed for currency in addition to trade goods. *Manillas* (brass bracelets) were used in the eastern Niger Delta, cowries were used on the slave coast and Guinea cloth was used on the Senegal River. In other areas, cloth, beads, iron bars, brass rods, brass bowls, alcohol, tobacco, guns and gunpowder were used. Much of the early cotton sold in the slave trade originated from India and the East Indies, though Europeans attempted to reproduce the cloth — not always successfully. However, some of the cloth used in trade came from Africa itself: Benin, Ijebu and southern Nigeria. The well-known "quaqua" cloth came from the Ivory Coast. Cloth from the Gambia and "high cloths" woven in the Cape Verde Islands by Afro-Portuguese were also bartered. Although the use of African cloth in slave trading declined in the eighteenth century, it was still traded after the abolition of the slave trade.

Beads were popular items of trade. The demand for them was subject to changes in fashion, and the type of beads desired differed from locale to locale. Some local beads known as aggrey beads were much prized on the Gold Coast. Iron bars were important items of trade and became a unit of currency in the Senegambia. Imported iron was often superior to the local product and was made into hoes and knives. Many knives were imported and the larger ones, variously known as cutlasses and machetes, were used as farming tools. Brass bracelets and bowls were in demand for household and ritual purposes. Alcohol was important to trade, but the quantities involved were small until the late eighteenth century. Whisky was used for paying commissions, dues, gifts and bribes, and was included in the price paid for slaves. Firearms and gunpowder became significant items of trade around the middle of the seventeenth century at the time of large-scale slave exports. Gold figured prominently in the trade. Although gold mined in Brazil by law had to be sent to Lisbon, large amounts were smuggled to West Africa, particularly to Whydah, to buy slaves.

While the demand for items varied from area to area, an assortment of goods was often involved in the purchase of a slave, so slave prices over longer periods are not easy to assemble.[47] But the evidence from recent research indicates that slave prices in West Africa rose during the period of the slave trade. The price paid for a male slave between the 1660s and the 1690s ranged from £3-4 sterling and increased to about £10 in 1700. The price reached about £18 in the 1730s but the cost declined somewhat and did not reach the 1730 peak again until the last quarter of the eighteenth century.[48] Prices for slaves further increased after British abolition because of the new risk involved in the trade;[49] but during the period of the slave trade prices did not always rise uninterruptedly but were affected by European wars and increases in shipping costs, as well as market demand in the Americas. Goods used to purchase slaves were quoted not in regular currency but rather in what was known as "commodity" currency, which permitted the exchange of slaves for a variety of goods on a one-to-one ratio. The value of goods paid for slaves in this manner was known as an ounce or a piece, and as the value of slaves rose, the goods that made up the "ounce" or "piece" correspondingly increased.[50]

Traders sometimes were dishonest, and both Africans and Europeans were constantly on guard against cheating. A slave-ship captain comments:

Not an article that is capable of diminution or adulteration, is delivered genuine, or entire. The spirits are lowered by water. False heads are put into the kegs that contain the gun powder; so that, though the keg appears large there is not more powder in it, than in a much smaller one. The linen and cotton cloths are opened, and two or three yards, according to the length of the piece, cut off, not from the end, but out of the middle, where it is not readily noticed. The natives are cheated, in the number, weight, measure, or quality of what they purchase, in every possible way; and by habit and emulation, a marvellous dexterity is acquired in these practices. And thus the natives in their turn, in proportion to their commerce with the Europeans, and (I am sorry to add) particularly with the English, become jealous, insidious and revengeful.[51]

When slaves were brought to be sold, they were carefully examined from head to foot, without regard to sex, to see that they did not have any blemish or defect:

A careful manipulation of the chief muscles, joints, armpits and groins was made, to assure soundness. The mouth, too, was inspected, and if a tooth was missing, it was noted as a defect liable to deduction. Eyes, voice, lungs, fingers, and toes were not forgotten; so that when the negro passed from the Mongo's hands without censure, he might have been readily adopted as a good "life" by an insurance company.[52]

William Bosman writes:

When the slaves which are brought from the inland countries come to Whidah, they are put in prison together, when we treat concerning buying them, they are all brought out together in a large plain, where, by our surgeons, they are thoroughly examined, and that naked both men and women, without the least distinction or modesty. Those which are approved as good are set on one side; in the meanwhile a burning iron, with the arm or name of the company, lies in the fire, with which ours are marked on the breast when we have agreed with the owners of the slaves they are returned to their prisons, where, from that time forward, they are kept at our charge, and cost us two pence a day each slave, which serves to subsist them like criminals on bread and water.[53]

The slaves were rejected if any defects were discovered on them. In some instances, the purchaser was free to return the slave the following morning if a defect was found upon re-examination. Rejected slaves were often severely beaten by their masters, and in places such as New Calabar were frequently put to death. However, most of these slaves became domestics; on the Gold Coast, they were known as *Wawa* (left ones).

Slavers seldom purchased Africans under 14 years old. The average age was between 14 and 35, although occasionally slaves older than 35 were sold. John Newton estimated that about two-thirds of a slave cargo were males,[54] and this predominance of men in the trade reinforced the probability that they were war captives. The young people and women were probably the result of kidnapping and raids. The social and economic value of women as potential wives and as agricultural labour in areas where women provided most of the work force may have accounted for their smaller numbers.

By 1788, traders estimated that from three weeks to three months of trading were needed to load a cargo of 450 slaves. There were, of course, regional variations. The typical duration of trading by slaving vessels in Sierra Leone ranged from four to nine months; on the Gold Coast trading time ranged from six to ten months. The efficiency of slave delivery varied from place to place. Supplying slave vessels with slaves was most efficiently carried out at Angola, followed by the Niger Delta, notably Bonny, and the Gold Coast.

Slaves from various regions were preferred for different reasons. According to John Atkins:

> Slaves differ in their goodness; those from the Gold Coast are accounted best, being cleanest limbed and more docile by our settlement than others; but then they are, for that very reason, more prompt to revenge, and murder the instruments of their slavery, and also apter in the means to compass it. To the Windward they approach in Goodness as is the distance from the Gold Coast; so as, at Gambia, or Sierra Leone, to be much better, than at any of the interjacent places. To Leeward from thence, they alter gradually for the worse; an Angolan negro is a proverb for worthlessness; and they mend in that way till you come to the Hottentots.[55]

West Indian planters also preferred slaves from certain regions. The French and Spaniards liked Yorubas from the Bight of Benin, and the English preferred Akans from the Gold Coast — known as "Coromantees" after the fort built at Cormantine in 1631 from which they were shipped. However, as demand and cost of slaves increased, planters could no longer afford the luxury of choice.

3
The Middle Passage

A few days before embarking on the ships, all slaves — male and female — had their heads shaved. When the cargo belonged to several owners, differentiating brands had to be impressed on the bodies of the Africans, using pieces of silver wire or small irons fashioned into the owner's initials. Portuguese traders baptized their slaves before transporting them, since it was forbidden under pain of excommunication to carry any slaves to Brazil who had not been christened.

On the day of departure for the New World, the slaves who had been confined to slave castles, *barracoons*, slave pens or the "houses" that the sailors constructed on deck were given an abundant meal,[1] which signalled the last hours in their homeland. After being fed, the Africans were taken to the slave vessels chained in pairs by the ankles. They were stripped naked when they boarded ship (European slave-traders justified this practice on the grounds that nudity was the only means of ensuring cleanliness and health during the voyage), and in this condition men and women were put into separate holds. The women and the boys, however, were often allowed to remain on deck, their only protection from the elements being a sail in fair weather and a tarpaulin in inclement weather.

There are few personal accounts describing the emotions of those who were placed on board the slave ships. Olaudah Equiano is one who has left us his reaction to this experience:

> The first object which saluted my eyes when I arrived on the coast was the sea, and a slave ship which was then riding at anchor and waiting for its cargo. These filled me with astonishment, which was soon converted into terror when I was carried on board. I was immediately handled and tossed up to see if I were sound by some of the crew, and I was now persuaded that I had gotten into a world of bad spirits and that they were going to kill me. Their complexions too differing so much

from ours, their hair and the language they spoke (which was very different from any I had ever heard) united to confirm me in this belief. Indeed such were the horrors of my views and fears at the moment that, if ten thousand worlds had been my own, I would have freely parted with them all to have exchanged my condition with that of the meanest slave in my own country. When I looked around the ship too and saw a large furnace of copper boiling, and a multitude of black people of every description chained together, every one of their countenances expressing dejection and sorrow, I no longer doubted of my fate; and quite overpowered with horror and anguish, I fell motionless on the deck and fainted.[2]

Most slaves understandably showed extreme distress and despair at being torn away from their homeland and dread of what came to be known as the Middle Passage. Some feared that they were being taken away to be eaten by their captors; the attempts by some slavers to explain to the victims the purpose for which they had been purchased failed to allay their fears.

The slavers of various countries often accused one another of keeping slovenly and foul ships. In truth, conditions on slave ships among the European powers were similar. The height of the decks averaged between four and five feet. In addition to the slave holds, some slavers built half-decks along the sides of the ship, extending no farther than the sides of scuttles where slaves, lying in two rows, one above the other, were crowded together. The males remained fastened by leg-irons in pairs. The women and children were usually free to move about as soon as the ship set sail. Where the behaviour of the male slaves warranted it, they were freed from their fastenings before they arrived in the New World. Brazilian slavers often dispensed with leg-irons when shipping the so-called "mild" blacks from Benin and Angola. Since it was known that a slave in irons deteriorated more rapidly, some slavers dispensed with irons when it was practical (from their perspective) to do so.

Slaves were brought up on deck at eight o'clock in the morning. Their irons were examined and a long chain locked to a ring fixed in the deck was run through the rings of the shackles of the men and locked to another ring-bolt fixed in the deck. In this way, sixty or more slaves could be fastened to the chains to prevent attempts at rebellion. They were given water with which to wash, and the ship's surgeon then examined them for sores or other ailments. Those who were ill were taken to a special section of the boat where they were treated.

Meals were served twice daily: breakfast around ten a.m. and another meal at four in the afternoon. The diet usually included rice, farina, yams and horse beans; on rare occasions, bran might be included. Some slavers offered their captives a so-called "African meal" once a day, followed in the evening by a European meal which consisted of horse beans boiled into a pulp. Most African slaves hated this dish so much that they would throw it overboard unless closely watched while eating. Slaves from various regions had their own food preferences. Those from the Windward Coast preferred rice, while those from the Niger Delta and Angola preferred manioc, although this was bulky and could not be kept long, so was not always available. A sauce was composed of palm oil mixed with water, and pepper was sometimes added to the food; the sailors called this mixture "slabber-sauce". The slaves were given half a pint of water twice a day. On some occasions pipes and tobacco were circulated, giving them a few puffs each. The slaves ate in groups and in good weather meals were taken on the deck; in bad weather, in the hold. It was usual to make the slave gang say grace before each meal and give thanks afterwards. After meals, a bucket of salt water was passed for washing hands.

In order to control the hungry captives' food consumption the process of eating was sometimes directed by signals from a monitor, who indicated when the slaves should dip their fingers or wooden spoons into the food and when they should swallow. It was the responsibility of the monitor to report those who refused to eat, and any slaves found to be attempting to starve themselves were severely whipped. There were instances in which hot coals were put on a shovel and placed so near the lips of a recalcitrant slave that his mouth was scorched and burned. At other times, the *speculum orum*, a mouth opener, was used to force food down a slave's throat.

Log books were kept of the ship's provisions. These records were vital, since the vessel's capacity did not allow for emergency provisions. When inclement weather prolonged the Middle Passage, food and water allowances were reduced. In 1781, the slave ship *Zong*, headed for Jamaica, ran short of water and food while also having an outbreak of disease. When the captain saw impending disaster, he proposed jettisoning those slaves who were too sick to recover, reasoning that the insurance underwriters, rather than the owners, would bear the loss. He further argued that the action would save slaves from lingering deaths. One hundred and thirty-six slaves were dragged to the deck and flung overboard. However, the underwriters of the policy refused to bear the loss. Although hundreds of slaves died from malnutrition, no efforts were made to recoup from the insurers, for the insurance law of the time stated:

> The insurer takes upon him the risk of the loss, capture, and death of slaves, or any other unavoidable accident to them; but natural death is always understood to be expected: by natural death is meant, not only when it happens by disease or sickness, but also when the captive destroys himself through despair, which often happens: but when slaves were killed, or thrown into the sea in order to quell an insurrection on their part, then the insurers must answer.[3]

In good weather, the daily morning routine included an opportunity for the slaves to wash and anoint themselves with oil. In the afternoon, they were forced to amuse themselves with singing and dancing, making music on a drum or on the bottom of a tub. Their songs were mostly lamentations of exile from their homeland. The singing and dancing were viewed in part as needed exercise during the voyage. Normally, the men who were confined in irons were ordered to stand up and make whatever motion they could. Those not chained danced around the deck. Slaves who did not relish the idea of exercising were compelled to do so by the lash of the whip. To help female slaves pass the time, some captains provided them with coloured beads and thread on which to string them. At six o'clock in the evening, the men were sent below deck. The women and children were allowed to remain above the deck longer if the weather permitted.

In most cases, the seamen were allowed to have sexual intercourse with the females. Officers were always permitted access to the women. Slaves who refused such advances were often severely beaten. A former slave-ship captain records:

> . . . the enormities frequently committed in an African ship, though equally flagrant, are little known *here*, and are considered *there*, only as

a matter of course. When the women and girls are taken on board a ship, naked, trembling, terrified, perhaps almost exhausted with cold, fatigue, and hunger, they are often exposed to the wanton rudeness of white savages. The poor creatures cannot understand the language they hear, but the looks and manner of the speakers are sufficiently intelligible. In imagination, the prey is divided, upon the spot, and only reserved till opportunity offers. Where resistance or refusal would be utterly in vain, even the solicitation of consent is seldom thought of.[4]

Although the regulations of the largest eighteenth-century Dutch slaving company, the Middleburg Commercial Company, forbade sexual harassment of female slaves, it is doubtful that sexually hungry sailors abided by this regulation.

At sundown, the second mate and boatswain went down to the hold, whip in hand, to arrange the slaves for sleep. In allocating places, particular attention was paid to size. The taller slaves were placed in the area of the greatest breadth of the vessel while those who were shorter were lodged near the bow. The slaves on the right-hand side of the vessel faced forward and lay in each others' laps, while those on the left faced the stern. In this manner, the slaves lay on their right sides, which certain slavers believed was good for the heart. Most slaves slept on bare boards, though some Portuguese slavers provided coarse mats. Often one out of every ten slaves was appointed to maintain order and silence at night and to enforce his commands was furnished with a "cat". This instrument, commonly used for flogging, consisted of a handle or stem, made of a rope three and a half inches in circumference and eighteen inches in length, at one end of which were fastened nine branches or tails made of log line, with three or more knots on each branch. In return for his service, this slave was often given an old shirt and a pair of trousers. Once a week, the ship's barber shaved heads and pared nails in order to prevent injuries during the nightly battles for sleeping space. Buckets were placed in each sleeping compartment to be used as latrines, though one can imagine that the chained slaves had difficulty reaching these in the dark of night.

The prevalence of disease at sea required that captains maintain some measure of cleanliness and employ a ship's surgeon. Slave cargoes were afflicted by fevers, dysentery and smallpox — smallpox being particularly disastrous, since there was no cure. At intervals, the slaves had their mouths rinsed with vinegar or lime juice, and were given a dram of the juice as an antidote to scurvy. To these health dangers were added the torments of seasickness and the oppressive heat in the holds. Ventilation was provided by about half a dozen portholes on either side of the ship. The hatches and bulkheads of slaving ships had grates, with openings cut above the deck for ventilation. When stifling tropical air in the hold made ventilation difficult at night, the gratings were removed and some of the slaves were allowed on the deck. In rainy weather when the gratings were covered, the slaves nearly suffocated.

Sick slaves were often placed under the half-deck where they slept on planks. At dawn, the surgeon would frequently find several slaves dead, still fastened to the living by their leg-irons. The practice of throwing dead slaves overboard brought sharks from miles around to feed on the bodies. Those slaves lacking the will to live often found ways to end their agonies. Women used cotton skirts as rope with which to hang themselves; other slaves jumped overboard when sentries were not vigilant.

The fear of slave mutinies led to strict controls, and intractable captives were severely punished. Although all would have welcomed the opportunity to escape, slaves from certain areas earned a reputation for rebellion. The so-called "Coromantees" of the Gold Coast were particularly known for their pride and mutinous behaviour. Apparently, the desperate fear of being eaten by whites on the other side of the Atlantic helped provoke mutiny. Often, the slaves sought to kill the European traders and set the vessel ashore. Slavers went to great lengths to prevent rebellions and mutinies, visiting the holds daily and searching every corner between decks for pieces of iron, wood or knives gathered by the slaves. Great care was taken not to leave lying about any object that could be used as a weapon. The yearning of slaves for their homelands led inevitably to rebellious attempts to gain liberty.

Mortality

By 1790, instead of a flat percentage, traders were paying premiums to slave captains according to the mortality rate of their cargo. The sum of £100 was paid to the master and £50 to the surgeon on each cargo when the ship's mortality rate was less than

2 per cent, and one half this amount if the mortality was between 2 per cent and 3 per cent. These figures are somewhat deceptive, because it was possible for captains and surgeons to misrepresent their actual losses by lying about the size of their original cargo in order to qualify for a premium. Thus, low percentages might be related more to the desire to secure premiums than to actual evidence of mortality. The Doblen's Act of 1788 reduced the person-to-tonnage ratio of slave ships, requiring a ratio of five slaves per three tons for ships up to 200 tons, and one slave per ton after that. Unfortunately, this act did not affect overcrowding, since a slave-ship owner often changed the registered tonnage of his ship without regard for its actual size.

Much has been written about "tight packers" and "loose-packers" in terms of how conditions differed according to the number of slaves loaded in a ship. However, recent research indicates that the mortality rate did not correlate to the number of slaves shipped per ton.[5] Although the number per ton was higher on vessels of less than 149 tons than on ships of greater size, they all experienced a similar death rate. The time-span of the voyage and the danger of resultant contagious disease probably had more effect on mortality than overcrowding. Thus, the distances from Africa to the New World are pertinent: from Gambia to the West Indies, 3,200 miles; from Sierra Leone, 4,000 miles; from the Gold Coast and the Niger Delta, 5,500 miles; from Angola, over 6,000 miles. Jamaica and Barbados were over 1,000 miles farther from West Africa than were the Leeward and Windward Islands. The duration of the Middle Passage from the major parts of West Africa averaged 60 days, with a large number of vessels completing the voyage within 40-69 days.

The reduced rations sometimes necessary during long voyages lowered the resistance of both slaves and crew. Given the varying incubation periods for disease, the longer the voyage the greater the chance of illness and death. Of the 60,783 slaves who were carried on 249 vessels of the Royal African Company between 1680 and 1688, only 45,396 survived the voyage. This figure represented a total mortality rate of approximately 24 per cent. Although initially the death rate was exceedingly high, during the later years of the trade mortality diminished. In the 1790s, the mortality rate for a

total of 522 vessels trading in West Africa was 6.6 per cent.

A recent study of the Middle Passage between 1790 and 1797 shows that mortality from most regions of West Africa was about 2.4 per cent to 5.1 per cent for the Gold Coast, with 10 per cent of the ships experiencing no mortality; 3.4 per cent for Angola, with 8.2 per cent of the ships experiencing no mortality; 3.9 per cent for Sierra Leone, with 5 per cent experiencing no mortality, and 9.7 per cent for the Niger Delta, with 2.7 per cent arriving with cargo intact. There were, however, ships as late as the 1790s that had death rates ranging from 18 per cent to an appalling 52 per cent.[6]

A recent study of the Dutch slave trade [7] indicates that between 1596-1650 the mortality rate was approximately 17 per cent. The rate dipped slightly for the West Indian Company and rose somewhat during the "free trade" period because of the greater length of time taken by independent traders to complete their cargos. This study concludes that men died at a higher rate than women: 19 per cent as compared to 14.7 per cent. Youths appear to have succumbed at the same rate as older men. This might be explained by the fact that the slave cargoes contained a higher percentage of boys. What data on slave mortality suggests is that it was not so much overcrowding of slave vessels or the inhumane treatment of slaves that caused the greatest loss of life during the Middle Passage but factors like disease and the length of the voyage.

Although death among the crews on the slavers did not exceed that of the slaves, there was a correlation which suggests that they were subject to similar conditions of disease, faulty provisions and length of voyage. However, available evidence suggests that only 30–34 per cent of the deaths of crew took place during the Middle Passage, with more than half of the deaths occurring while the vessel was on the African coast, presumably because of climate, disease, and addiction to alcohol and other vices. Day and night, seamen were exposed to wind and sea. They were forced to sleep on deck, exposed to all types of weather, an old tarpaulin thrown over a boom being their only shelter. This exposure frequently caused illness and death. Seamen were issued three pounds of bread per man, an insufficient ration meant to last through the week. They were allowed three pounds per week of pork or beef, which might be reduced to half that weight after cooking, since it was mostly fat and bone. Often, the crew was given only one meal a day, and because they were the first to be deprived when there was a shortage of provisions, it was common for sailors to beg rations from the slaves. Provisions were commonly refused to sick sailors: on many slavers, the rule was "no work, no victuals". Crew members often had access to fresh water only through the bunghole of the water barrel using a gun barrel as a drinking straw. To discourage waste, the gun barrel was fastened to the topmast and a thirsty sailor was forced to climb up and retrieve the gun barrel and return it after securing his drink. On some slave ships, every eight sailors were given a pint of brandy to share once or twice a month.

For the Middle Passage, there were generally ten sailors to every 100 slaves. Once the ship unloaded its human cargo, however, there was no need for a large crew on the return journey to Europe. As a result, crews were often deliberately maltreated to encourage them to desert. Thomas Clarkson studied the muster of 83 slavers which sailed between August 1786 and September 1787, noting the numbers of the original crew, those returning with the ship, those dead or lost and those discharged. Of 3,170 men, 1,428 returned to Europe, 642 died and 1,000 deserted. Once ashore, many seamen died from alcohol, which their debilitated bodies were unable to tolerate.

Sale of slaves

Ships taking slaves to the West Indies often touched the island of St Thomas, or Princess Island, where the sick were taken ashore to recuperate and the supply of water was replenished. Captains preferred to sell their slave cargoes at a single island port. However, when the prices were unattractive or all the slaves could not be sold, slave captains might peddle them in small quantities from island to island.

On arrival, slavers had three ways of selling their cargo: private treaty, "scramble" and public auction. By private treaty, slaves were sold either directly to planters or to specialized wholesalers at an established price. During the early stage of the trade, island merchants served as agents to sell slaves to the planters on commission. Later, the merchants traded for themselves, buying from the slave ships and reselling the slaves to the planters. Slaves sold by public auction were often sickly; therefore the prices they fetched were naturally low. Various methods were used to get high prices for sickly slaves. Some slave captains directed the surgeons on their boats to stuff the anuses of those afflicted with the flux with oakum before they were landed for sale.

During the early years of slave trade to the West Indies, the payment for slaves was made in sugar or rum. Later this was changed and bills of exchange were usually drawn on the account of the merchant to whom the planter consigned his sugar; sometimes a combination payment in sugar, rum and bills was used. The transition from sugar to bills of exchange as a method of payment was caused by the increase in slave prices in terms of the value of sugar, which made it impossible for ships to carry a cargo of sugar equal to the value of a cargo of slaves. The slave-trading activities of Europeans and Africans, the transportation of the slaves to the Americas and their sale to slave holders was a brutal and dehumanizing experience, which persisted for so long because of the labour needs of the New World.

4
Demand, Supply and Distribution

African slaves had reached Europe and beyond through the trans-Saharan trade centuries before the Atlantic slave trade began. Until the fifteenth century, an active slave trade existed between the Mediterranean area, the regions of central Europe and the Black Sea area.[1] Although some African slaves had reached southern Europe earlier, the Portuguese voyages of exploration initiated a regular trade in slaves by sea between Africa and Europe. This commerce later developed into the transatlantic slave trade between Africa and the Americas. The bulk of these slaves who came to the New World were used on sugar, tobacco, cotton and coffee plantations. Some of the slaves were also employed in mining activities.

The volume of Africans involved in this trade has been the subject of a lively debate. According to a recent estimate based on the work of the pioneering efforts of Philip Curtin and the work of other scholars in the field, Paul Lovejoy has estimated that Africa exported some 11,698,000 people in the Atlantic slave trade and that 9,778,500 of them landed in the New World. Lovejoy's figures are remarkably close to Curtin's original findings. The revised figures of slave imports into the Americas and the Atlantic basin breaks down as follows: 293,400 slaves imported from 1451-1600; 1,494,600 imported from 1601-1700; 5,737,600 imported in 1701-1810.[2] The large import of slaves into the Americas was part of what has been described as the expansion of the European capitalistic economy that began during the late fifteenth century, drawing labourers from Africa and capital and managerial skills from Europe to produce and extract wealth from the New World.[3]

The largest influx of Africans involved in the early slave trade with Europe from the fifteenth to the seventeenth centuries went to Portugal and Spain.[4] Slaves were also found during this period in Italy (in Naples), in Holland (Amsterdam), and in France (Nantes and Bordeaux). Following Phillip II's assumption of the Portuguese throne in 1580, Lisbon became an important centre for the slave trade and many Africans who were brought there were re-exported to Andalusian cities and other parts of Spain. Seville, Cordoba, Malaga, Granada and Cadiz had large numbers of black slaves, most of whom were engaged in domestic work. Following the Portuguese War for Independence, after 1640, the Portuguese suspended licences to supply the Spaniards with slaves.

An exact accounting of slave imports to Spain and Europe from the fifteenth to the seventeenth centuries is impossible. However, Curtin's data show that, on the basis of fifteenth- and sixteenth-century reports from the Lisbon customs house, there were approximately 50,000 imports for the period of the slave trade.[5] About eighty per cent of these were owned by the aristocracy, clergy or officials.

The decrease in the number of Africans imported to Europe was related to development in the New World following the voyages of exploration by Christopher Columbus in the 1490s and the emergence of the use of African slaves in the Americas.

The Iberian colonies

During the late fifteenth century and the early decades of the sixteenth, Spain established permanent settlements in Hispaniola, Puerto Rico, Jamaica, Cuba, the coast of Venezuela and the Darien-Panama area. Under Hernán Cortés, they conquered the Aztec Empire in Mexico between 1519-22 and were in control of the areas of present-day Guatemala and El Salvador by 1524. Under Francisco Pizarro, the Inca Empire of Peru was conquered in 1532-3. The Spanish presence extended from the area north of Quito to modern Colombia, Venezuela and the Bolivian Plateau.

The early Spanish settlers were motivated by prospects of economic gain. The most powerful attraction was gold, and the majority of the Spaniards who went first to the Caribbean island of Hispaniola spent their time seeking the precious metal and then moving on to other islands and the mainland to continue the search. The indigenous Indian population was called upon to perform the task of working the gold mines and providing labour for other economic activities. In these areas of settlement, Spain established a provisional form of government centred on a system of *encomiendas*, which were labour and tribute grants. The individual granted the *encomienda* was given the responsibility for protecting the resident Indians, and in turn received labour and tribute from them. The brutal mine work, for which the Indians were not adapted, took a tremendous toll; and their lack of immunity toward European diseases such as smallpox, typhus, measles, influenza and syphilis cruelly increased their mortality rate.

It has been estimated that the Western hemisphere contained 80-100 million inhabitants before the European conquest of the region, with only 10 million inhabitants left after the first century of European colonization.[6] Mexico had an estimated population of 20 million in 1519, which was reduced to 1,069,255 by 1608. Hispaniola had a population of 60,000 Amerindians in 1508, 30,000 in 1554, and 500 in 1570.[7] If these demographic estimates are correct, the impact of European conquest and the ravages of disease upon Amerindians exceeded by far the worst ravages of the Atlantic slave trade upon the African peoples.

As the population of Amerindians declined, their labour functions were transferred to African slaves. Some Spaniards who came to the New World brought slaves with them as servants or companions. It is believed that some blacks accompanied Columbus on his voyages to the New World and that Alfonso Pietro, the pilot of *La Nina*, was black. Black slaves came with the Spanish conquistadors and became a medium of exchange anywhere Spanish armies were found. Conquistadors such as Hernán Cortés and Francisco Pizarro were given permission to import African slaves from 1529 to 1537. Other pioneers and conquerors in Latin America enjoyed the same privileges. In the course of the sixteenth century, officials such as viceroys, governors, judges and parish priests were allowed to take three to eight slaves with them to the New World without the licences which normally regulated the import of slaves. Because of the need for black military assistance, the conquistadors were granted certain privileges in relation to their slaves. During the early part of the conquest, slaves were used as companions and assistants, rather than as brute labour force. Black freedmen also served as intermediaries, overseers and managers.

They, as well as the Spaniards, met resistance from the Amerindians, who did not differentiate between them. Black slaves often assisted their masters with conquering and subjugating the Indians during the early period of Spanish settlement. Many of the slaves earned their freedom and some became slave holders.

By the middle of the sixteenth century, blacks had spread to all the parts of South America visited or controlled by Europeans. By the mid-seventeenth century, the distribution of blacks in the New World had become stabilized. The early Spanish settlers emphasized that black labour was needed for producing goods essential to European colonization. Blacks were preferred for work in the gold mines: Europeans argued that the work output of one African was equal to that of four to eight Indians and that the use of blacks would alleviate the suffering of the indigenous population.

The introduction of tropical crops, such as sugar, and the depletion of the Indian population led to the increased importation of African slaves. The production of sugar in large quantities required a substantial initial capital outlay and a large, controlled labour force for growing and processing. By 1509, the first sugar mills in Spanish America were opened, and in 1523 twenty-four mills were operating.

Just when there was an increasing need for labour, Spain, who had no forts on the African coast, granted special licences known as *asientos* to certain of her subjects for the importation of slaves. With Spanish churchmen interceding on behalf of Indians who were perishing from disease and overwork, the Spanish crown began to turn to Africa as a source of labour. The organized importation of slaves directly from Africa began in 1518, when Charles I of Spain granted to a member of his household known as Lorenzo de Gomenot, Duke of Bresa, an *asiento* which allowed 4,000 African-born slaves (*bonzles*) a year to be imported into Hispaniola, Cuba, Jamaica and Puerto Rico. Gomenot sold his permit to some Genoese merchants who, in turn, sold the licence to the Portuguese.[8]

For the rest of the sixteenth century, various individuals and groups were licensed to supply labourers for the New World. As the demand for black slaves increased, Spanish kings charged exorbitant prices for these licences. From 1580 to 1640, the Portuguese dominated the *asientos*, which were suspended between 1640 and 1663 because of the Portuguese revolt for independence against Spain. Licences were also withheld from the Dutch, who had been encroaching upon Spanish territory and were regarded as heretics and rebels, and from the French and Danes, regarded as weak and unable to hand the *asiento* contracts with security. After 1663 the licences were given to an assortment of merchants or merchant houses from Portugal, the Netherlands, Genoa and Venice. The *asientos* became a great international prize, and wars were fought in order to secure rights to supply slaves to the Spanish colonies.

Slaves delivered by these contracts were defined in terms of their labour potential and were often young people meeting specific conditions of physique and health. They were valued in terms of a unit known as *piezas de India*, or *peca de India*, the definition of which changed over a period of time, but in the middle of the seventeenth century healthy slaves aged between 15 and 25 passed the test for a *peca de India*; if the slaves were aged between 8 and 15 or 25 and 35, then three of them were regarded as two *peca de India*.[9]

Because the licences were granted in *peca de India* rather than in terms of number of slaves, it is not easy to determine the true figure for slaves landed in Spanish America during this period. The calculation is further complicated by the fact that licence holders often filled their ships with other profitable cargo, replacing some of the slaves on the manifest. The desire to smuggle goods other than slaves led to figures being inflated in collusion with corrupt customs-house officers in Spanish America. A recent study, using the *asientos* as a guide, has suggested that between 1714 and 1739 the South Sea Company, which was active in distributing slaves in Spanish America, brought about 140,800 Africans to the Spanish colonies. During the years 1641-1773, Spanish America received an annual average of 3,880 slaves.[10]

Spain stopped granting general *asientos* after 1773, making it hard to assess the number of slaves subsequently imported. After 1773, Spanish flagships and French, Dutch, Danish and North American slavers carried Africans directly to the Spanish colonies. Spain also bought slaves from the Plata basin, Jamaica and other British colonies. In some areas of the Spanish Caribbean the problem was compounded by the difficulty of estimating numbers needed in various areas for full productive capacity and the number needed to replace decreasing slave populations where the mortality rate was high.

In spite of the early Spanish settlement on Cuba, the use of slave labour for the island's sugar economy did not expand until towards the end of the eighteenth century. Much of the Spanish slave cargo from 1774-1807 went to Cuba after it started to experience a spectacular growth of sugar plantations. This expansion and Cuba's need for slaves continued during much of the nineteenth century. It is estimated that by 1870 Cuban sugar exports accounted for over one-third of the world's estimated sugar-cane production. This voluminous output was made possible by the shifting of slaves already on the island from urban employment, production of tobacco, coffee and by the importation of additional slaves from Africa during the nineteenth century.[11] The general pattern of slave importation to the Spanish colonies followed the needs of labour, except in areas with large Indian populations. Although Indians were generally used in mining activities, blacks did not escape this type of activity, and large numbers worked in the gold mines of Peru, Venezuela and Chile, but not in the silver mines of Bolivia since the cool, arid climate of the area was considered unhealthy for them. In addition to employment in the sugar-cane fields of Mexico, Colombia, Peru and the Antilles, African slaves were used to produce cocoa in Venezuela, grapes and olives in south-central Peru and wheat in Chile.

Portuguese colonies

Brazil was sighted by Pedro Alvares Cabral of Portugal in 1500. During the early part of the sixteenth century, the French organized expeditions along the coast of Brazil to promote settlements to attack the Iberian colonies. This threat from France led Portugal to promote a systematic colonization of the area, and sugar became the primary export crop during the sixteenth century.

Portuguese sugar cultivation in the New World was preceded by some decades of similar cultivation on the Atlantic islands off Africa, including Madeira, the Azores, Cape Verde Islands and São

Tomé, and black slaves were employed in these endeavours.[12] The cultivation of sugar in these islands helped the future development of the Brazilian plantations by providing experience and expertise on technical problems related to production. The use of slaves on sugar plantations in these islands was well established, and the practice was extended to new settlements in Brazil.

Sugar became big business in the New World. Although sugar plantations developed in Hispaniola, Puerto Rico and on plantations in Mexico, the high cost of production, local consumption and lack of investment capital and marketing problems kept down Spanish sugar exports. It was Brazil that became the main exporter, and this called for the large importation of black slaves, especially after 1550. The success of the Brazilian sugar industry was linked to natural conditions, available capital and the efficient marketing of sugar in Europe. In Brazil, excellent soil and adequate rainfall aided cultivation, while the proximity of ports to the sugar fields made the product easy to export. Marketing facilities available in Europe from the end of the fifteenth century offered optimal distribution to the growers. From the middle of the sixteenth century, Dutch merchants began to dominate the exportation of sugar from Brazil. During that time the Dutch were the only nation with the commercial organization and capital to finance the distribution of sugar. Dutch capital was also involved in importing slaves from Africa for the plantations.[13]

Between the sixteenth and the nineteenth centuries, Brazil imported some 3.5 million slaves from Africa, particularly into the region of Bahia, and with this manpower the sugar industry grew and prospered. The first sugar mills were established in São Vicente in 1533 and yielded about 50 tons of sugar a year. The steady growth of production was interrupted from 1630 to 1654, when the Dutch occupied northern Brazil. Since the Dutch had controlled much of the maritime trade and sugar marketing of Europe, they were not prepared to forego a substantial part of the sugar business when Spain conquered Portugal. The effort of the Dutch to control the sugar trade was one reason for the war they waged against Spain from 1580 to 1640.

The Dutch, who had no trading posts on the African coast when they seized Brazil, captured Elmina on the Gold Coast in 1637 and

Angola in 1641 in order to provide Brazil with slaves.[14] The period of Dutch occupation, while it disrupted Portuguese efforts, did not lead to a decline in sugar exports, for the Dutch strove to continue cultivation and export. During the period from 1629 to 1660 sugar exports reached their peak. After 1660, Brazil lost its position as the leading producer of sugar to Dutch, English and French plantations in the Caribbean. In effect, the entry of Northern Europeans into New World sugar production marked the decline of the Iberian monopoly.

The expertise gained by the Dutch in Brazil enabled them to establish sugar industries when they moved into the Caribbean from the mainland. The Dutch helped the French and British to establish themselves in the Caribbean, giving them technological aid and credit for equipment, slaves and land.

Sugar production in Brazil, with its attendant slave labour, continued after the Dutch were expelled. In addition to the plantations, other forms of economic activity necessitated slaves. The discovery of gold in Brazil in the 1690s and the early part of the eighteenth century called for workers in the mining areas.[15] To achieve a high and immediate return on investments, prospectors had to invest heavily in machinery and labour. Both skilled and unskilled labourers were employed, and miners engaged slave carpenters, masons and smiths. Substantial demand developed suddenly in the gold mines, leading to large increases in imports. While the numbers of slaves had increased gradually in plantation areas, demand rose sharply in the gold mines.

The rise of coffee cultivation brought another influx of slaves to Brazil during the nineteenth century. Coffee cultivation in southern Brazil was concentrated in substantial holdings that required large amounts of capital and credit. Like the sugar planters, coffee growers required reliable, efficient labour, and the nineteenth-century slave trade from Africa as well as internal slave-trading from northern to southern Brazil made the rapid expansion of coffee possible. In all, some 3.5 million Africans were imported into Brazil during the period of the slave trade.

Northern European colonies

Although the countries of Northern Europe made strenuous efforts to break the Spanish monopoly in the New World, these attempts ended in failure until the seventeenth century. That the Northern European countries were then able to acquire colonies was due in part to the weakened condition of Spanish military power during the first half of the seventeenth century, following the Anglo-Spanish War of 1585. The power of the Dutch, French and English had meanwhile grown to the extent that they could defy the Spanish monopoly. These acquired colonies developed into prosperous plantations during the ensuing two centuries.[16]

The British Caribbean

Of the colonies established by the Northern European countries during the seventeenth and eighteenth centuries, those of the English were by far the most successful.[17] From the late fifteenth century until the early part of the seventeenth century, the Spanish colonies in the West Indies were the only European settlements in the area. The islands of the West Indies, however, were of a lesser significance to the Spanish than were their mainland colonies such as Peru and Mexico. Although Spaniards had settled on some of the Greater Antilles, which had been said to produce tobacco and sugar, the smaller islands had essentially been left to the fierce Carib Indians. It was on these lesser islands that the English and other Europeans settled.

The English successfully settled in St Christopher in 1624, Barbados in 1627, Nevis in 1628, Montserrat and Antigua in 1632 and Jamaica in 1655. Prior to 1640, when the British Caribbean islands primarily grew tobacco, very few slaves were employed. This was because crops like tobacco were better suited to small-holdings rather than to big plantations which employed a large number of slaves. The number of slaves on the islands increased greatly, however, with the introduction of sugar. The successful cultivation of this crop after 1640 resulted in the rapid rise of a planter class in the islands. So successful was the English plantation effort that by 1700 English planters in Barbados, Jamaica and the Leeward Islands were supplying almost half of the sugar consumed in Europe. This, of course, was accomplished by the use of a slave system that drew labour from Africa.

Initially labour in the British colonies was performed by white indentured servants. During the seventeenth century, the lower-middle classes provided both temporary and permanent labour. Groups found their way to the British West Indies during the 1620s and 1630s, some voluntarily, others as kidnapped victims. Indentured servants bound themselves for four or five years and received some acreage of land in the colonies at the end of their service. Barbados, which was the first successful English sugar colony, attracted a large number of these servants. As time went on, however, the island developed a bad reputation for cruel conditions, and few people wanted to go there.

The use of black slaves in the British West Indies became predominant between 1640 and 1660, when crops were shifted from tobacco and cotton to sugar. The sugar boom of Barbados was reflected in land prices, which increased nearly tenfold in seven years, from 10 shillings per acre in 1640 to £5 in 1646.[18] As sugar prospered, land distribution on the island favoured large entrepreneurs, and small proprietors were eliminated. Sugar interests with plantations averaging about 200 acres acquired the best land; to make them productive they needed a permanent, reliable labour force.

When Barbados turned to the use of African slaves, the Spanish and Portuguese colonies had had a long experience with the use of slavery. However, English ethnocentricism and strong aversion to living among black people prevented their early adoption of the institution of slavery. But English attitudes towards black people changed when white labour proved unstable and the prices for procuring servants increased. Beyond the ideological reasons, Barbados was producing a commodity that called for heavy investments in sugar and was in a position to invest in slaves.

There was an additional factor which encouraged the use of Blacks in the British West Indies. Wage increases in England had raised the supply prices of indentured servants at a time when slave prices were falling.[19] Furthermore, planters from Barbados who had visited Pernambuco around 1640 to learn how to make sugar also discovered that Brazilian sugar plantations were manned by African slaves and that slavery had advantages over unstable white labour. The cost of African slaves, which had been about $25 in the 1640s, dropped to $15, making African slaves better value than white servants for white planters. In addition, Dutch traders were able to provide a regular supply of slaves to the planters at Barbados. Once these planters started using slaves on their sugar plantations they never looked back.

With the marriage of sugar and slavery, Barbados prospered. The soil was suited for sugar, and expansion of sugar plantations came at a time when the Portuguese and Dutch were embroiled in conflict over Brazil. Moreover, the Dutch, who showed the English the process of growing cane and making sugar, not only supplied the planters with slaves on easy terms but also sold English sugar on the continent at profitable prices. In spite of the great need for slaves during the eighteenth century, the demands of the various British colonies varied. By 1724, Barbados contained no land that had not been granted or was not under cultivation. The English plantation system in the British West Indies reached its peak during the eighteenth century, and a continuous supply of slave labour was essential for the continued prosperity of the islands. This inter-dependence of sugar and slavery was an accepted fact in the eighteenth century.

By 1730, while Barbados had adequate slave labour for her plantation activities, the other colonies were insufficiently supplied. Because of its vast areas of uncultivated land, the demand for slaves in Jamaica was keen.[20] The shortage of slaves on this island was blamed on the *asientos* of 1713 with Spain, which obligated the British to supply the Spanish colonies with 4,800 slaves a year. Jamaica became the depot for shipping slaves to the Spanish colonies. The ready payment offered by the Spaniards made that market more attractive than trade with resident British planters, who expected long periods of credit. In order to get enough labour for their needs, Jamaican planters attempted in 1732 to impose duties on slaves exported from the island. This, however, did not diminish the export to the Spanish colonies. After 1739, because of war with Spain and the lapse of the *asientos*, about a quarter of the slaves brought to Jamaica were re-exported, as opposed to one-third to one-half before that date.

Most of the slaves imported into the English colonies during the seventeenth century were supplied by the Dutch and the British, although there is little available evidence to support an analysis of the slave trade for the British Caribbean before 1663. After that period, however, the records of the Royal African Company (whose headquarters at Cape Coast castle could hold up to 1,500 captives awaiting shipment) are of some help in estimating imports. The number of slaves imported by the Royal African Company from 1663 to 1711 and by private traders from 1698 to 1707 amounted to 88,811 for Barbados, 75,510 for Jamaica and 21,424 for the Leeward Islands. Between 1663 and 1689, some 70 per cent of these slaves came from the Windward coast, the Gold Coast and the Slave Coast, and the rest from Senegambia and Angola.[21]

French colonies

French pirates and privateers were operating in the New World as early as 1504. It was not until the seventeenth century, however, that France acquired colonies there. The French occupied three islands in the West Indies, settling St Christopher, Guadeloupe and Martinique in 1635.[22] France secured St Domingue (San Domingo, the western part of Hispaniola) from the Spanish in 1697. With the acquisition of colonies, and after growing tobacco, indigo, cotton and ginger, the French, like the British, went over to sugar production. The need for labour for the sugar plantations led the French to organize monopolies to supply her colonies with slaves. From 1664, sugar became the primary export of the French West Indies, and it was this activity that transformed the colonies. In the process real-estate prices rocketed and, as with the British, small-holders were eventually dispossessed by large landowners.

The heart of French sugar production was in Martinique, Guadeloupe and St Domingue. As in other colonies in the Caribbean, investment in sugar called for a reliable labour force. Until the end of the seventeenth century, the French relied on indentured (*engagé*) labour, which was often recruited for a period of three years. As a result of this and the slow development of sugar production in the French Caribbean, there were few slaves on the French islands in 1700. In St Domingue, most planters owned no more than twelve slaves.

Successful sugar cultivation began in Guadeloupe and quickly expanded to Martinique, which became the leading producer of sugar in the French West Indies. By the 1740s St Domingue had become the most productive of the French colonies. At this time coffee was also grown there, but when the price of coffee fell the island returned to sugar production. At the pinnacle of its success as a sugar colony in 1791, the year of the black slave revolt, production had grown to 78,696 tons from 2,920 tons in 1710. Given the level of production in St Domingue, much of the French slave imports were to that colony.

The French were the third largest European slave-trading nation and accountable for a little over 20 per cent of African slaves imported to America. The majority of imports into the French colonies came from Angola and the Bight of Benin, with smaller numbers coming from the Bight of Biafra, the Gold Coast and Senegambia.

Dutch West Indies

The Dutch, as we have seen, took the early initiative in challenging the claims of Spain in the New World, and in the 1630s they took the islands of Curaçao, St Eustatius and Tobago in the Caribbean. Although they were prominent in the seventeenth-century slave trade and were still important carriers during the eighteenth century, most of the slaves the Dutch traded went to other European colonies.[23] Dutch settlements such as Curaçao and Aruba were more devoted to the slave trade than to agriculture. While Surinam, Demerara, Berbice and Essequibo went into sugar production they were not as successful as the islands of Barbados, Jamaica and St Domingue.

An analysis of the early years of the Dutch trade in terms of its size is difficult, given the present state of research, but there is enough evidence to make estimates for the late seventeenth and eighteenth centuries. The Dutch trade up to 1675 was small, and the slave imports have been estimated at 70,000. The most active era can be divided into two parts: the period from 1675 to 1735, during which the Dutch West India Company, with several forts on the African coast, maintained a monopoly, and the free-trade period from 1730 to 1795. The Dutch share of the slave trade at its peak was 10 per cent and, in total, the Dutch imported approximately 500,000 Africans. Curaçao was an important depot for slaves going to the Spanish colonies during the four decades the

Dutch held the *asientos*, from 1662 to 1713. Although St Eustatius briefly served as a slave depot, it was the development of her own plantations that brought large numbers of slaves to the colony in the 1760s and 1770s.

During the eighteenth century, 90 per cent of the slaves involved in Dutch free trade were shipped to Surinam, while 67 per cent of the Dutch West India Company's trade were sent there during the first three decades of the century. Of the slaves involved in the Dutch trade, 25 per cent came from the Loango-Angola coast and 75 per cent from various locations on the Guinea coast.

The Danish trade

The Danes, who in 1661 had taken Christiansborg Castle on the Gold Coast from the Dutch, made their appearance in the Caribbean in 1671, when Christian V of Denmark granted a charter to his subjects to establish plantations on the unoccupied islands of St Thomas and St John. From 1680 the work of planting sugar was vested in the Danish West India Company, but the Danish Crown took over this task in 1754. The progress of sugar on these islands was not spectacular, and by 1725 there were only about 4,490 slaves on St Thomas and 1,414 slaves on St John. The production of St Croix, which was purchased by the Danes in 1733, was also limited, and in 1754 there was a population of only 7,566 slaves. St Croix later became the largest of the Danish sugar islands. Some 53,000 slaves were imported for use on this island, of whom 50,000 were imported in Danish ships.

The North American colonies

In the British West Indian colonies, the problems of a suitable export crop and labour force were solved relatively early.[24] In the British North American colonies, which shared a similar climate with the mother country, it was not easy to find a profitable export crop that could pay for the cost of investment. The delay in finding a remunerative product for export slowed the development of these colonies. In the long term, however, it was the cultivation of tobacco, rice and later, cotton in the southern colonies that brought economic rewards and large numbers of black slaves to the country.

The need for adequate labour became clear as tobacco production increased from the seventeenth century through the eighteenth century. By 1627, the annual tobacco export of the colony amounted to £500,000. The colonists shipped £20 million in 1700, £80 million by the mid-1730s and £220 million in 1775. By the eighteenth century, Virginia and Maryland had responded to the difficulty in obtaining enough indentured servants by turning to slave labour.

The cultivation of rice in South Carolina relied upon the labour of black slaves. As a colony, South Carolina grew slowly until rice became a viable export crop in 1695. In two subsequent decades African slave imports equalled and surpassed the white populations, so that by 1708 Blacks in South Carolina were clearly in the majority.

Initially the European settlers of South Carolina had been unable to grow rice because they were unacquainted with its cultivation. The African slaves, however, knew how to plant the crop, since an indigenous variety of rice (*oryza blaberrima*) was grown in the rain-forests of Africa. In fact, rice grown in these areas had been used in provisioning slave ships headed for the Americas. Thus, it is believed that Negro slaves, who before 1700 faced shortages and had been encouraged to grow their own food, succeeded with rice crops where their masters had been unsuccessful. In addition to rice, the cultivation of indigo (blue dye) was introduced to the colony in 1742 and expanded after 1748.

While the use of slave labour allowed tobacco, rice and indigo to be produced profitably over a wide area, the total area of the South dedicated to plantations and the use of slaves remained small until a new "El Dorado" was discovered in cotton at the end of the eighteenth century. Eli Whitney's cotton gin overnight made the green-seed upland cotton a commercial crop. The rewards of growing cotton expanded the plantation region from the narrow confines of the coastlands to the rest of the South.

As in the British West Indies, there had been a transition from the use of indentured servants to the use of slaves in the British North American colonies. It was not until the 1690s, however, that slaves became cheaper than indentured labour. The first black people to arrive in North America came before the systematic importation of slaves began. As early as 1526, Lucas Vasquez de Ayllón, a Spanish official from Hispaniola, attempted to establish a colony in North America and landed 200 Spaniards and 100 black slaves near Cape Fear in North Carolina. The colony was unsuccessful and, although a remnant of the Spaniards returned to Hispaniola, the blacks remained and joined forces with the Indians.

The systematic importation of slaves into British North America was initiated by the Dutch in 1619, when they sold twenty slaves to the settlement at Jamestown. The first shipment of Africans to what was then called New Amsterdam (later New York) was in 1625. Until 1654 the Dutch dominated the supply of slave labour to the North American continent. Following the enactment of the Navigation Acts in 1651 and the establishment of English monopoly companies, the trade and supply of slaves became the business of British and American merchants.

There was a limited demand for slaves in North America until the end of the seventeenth century. The bulk of the slaves who came to Virginia up to 1680 were from the West Indies, especially Barbados. Although American merchants became interested in the Atlantic slave trade as early as 1643, very few slaves were delivered directly from Africa. The trade grew considerably after 1680, when the American colonies increasingly began to need labour and showed a preference for slaves from Africa. In 1710, the Virginia Council reported to the House of Burgesses:

> For as much as most of the Negroes imported for Her Majesty's Plantations are either such as are transported for crimes or infected with disease, the council submits to the consideration of your house whether it may not be proper that a higher duty be laid on them than on Negroes imported directly from Africa.[25]

Between 1698 and the outbreak of the American War of Independence in 1775, Newport, Boston and New York were the three major American ports for the slave trade. New London, Connecticut, Providence, Rhode Island, and Philadelphia were minor ports for the trade. The major American slave-trading ports between 1783 and 1807 were Newport, Boston and Charleston.

Sugar plantations were not a major factor in the slave trade to North America, since the emergence of sugar in Louisiana in 1795 did not come about until a decade before the slave trade to the United States was abolished. The spectacular growth of cotton in the Southern states also came mere years before the slave trade was abolished. Much of the labour needs for cotton and sugar in the nineteenth century, therefore, had to be met through natural propagation. The estimate for the total slave imports into the United States had been put at 596,000.[26] The bulk of these imports came from Angola, the Bight of Biafra, the Gold Coast and from Senegambia.

Whatever the destination of slaves in the New World, the purpose of their importation was economic. They were used on sugar, coffee, tobacco and cotton plantations; they were employed in other agricultural pursuits, such as growing rice in South Carolina, and they were used in mining enterprises. The demands of sugar plantations in particular, which called for sixteen to twenty hours of labour in the harvesting seasons, led to a high mortality rate among slaves, many of whom survived only eight to ten years. Some sugar planters periodically had to replace whole populations of slaves.

Gold mining, especially in Brazil, also exacted a heavy toll. Prospecting in icy streams seriously affected the blacks, who quickly deteriorated physically, and overwork and disease limited their life-span there to ten or twelve years. It is, therefore, not surprising that the largest number of imports went to the mining and sugar-growing areas of the Caribbean and Brazil. Brazil imported 38 per cent of the slaves who came from Africa, the British Caribbean 17 per cent, the French Caribbean 17 per cent, Spanish America 17 per cent, North America 6 per cent and the Dutch, Danish and Swedish Caribbean 6 per cent.

The demand and need that brought these Africans into the New World reached its peak during the eighteenth century. By then, however, changes in Europe and the New World were at work to abolish the trade and the institution of slavery that had brought Africans to the Americas as forced labour.

5
The End of Black Slavery

The abolition of the slave trade and slavery came at a time when religion, economics and philosophy pointed to the undesirable nature of slavery. The abolition movement, which should be viewed within the changing context of the prevailing economic climate of Europe and the Americas, may conveniently be divided into three parts. There were the efforts to abolish formally the slave trade. This was followed by Britain's diplomatic and naval actions to ensure that slaves were not exported. Last, there were the efforts to abolish slavery in the New World. The efforts to abolish slavery in British colonies were closely tied to reform movements of the period. The history of the abolition of slavery in the nineteenth century is part of the complex history of the individual nations and cannot be dealt with in any great detail here.

When the nations involved decided to end their participation in the slave trade, the factors governing their decisions were complex. As William Wilberforce, the English abolitionist, maintained: "In point of fact great political events are rarely the offspring of cool, deliberate systems; they receive their shape, size and colour, and the data of their existence, from a thousand causes which could hardly have been foreseen, and in the production of which, various unconnected and jarring parties have combined and assisted."[1] In spite of the complexities of the process, however, contemporaries viewed abolition of the slave trade as a humanitarian achievement. According to W. E. H. Lecky, "The unweary, unostentatious, and inglorious crusade of England against slavery may probably be regarded as among the three or four perfectly virtuous pages comprised in the history of nations."[2] Thomas Clarkson, in one of the early studies of British abolition, viewed the campaign to end the trade as a conflict between good and evil men. It was "a contest between those who felt deeply for the happiness and honour of their fellow-creatures and those who through vicious custom and the impulse of avarice, had trampled underfoot the sacred rights of their nature, and had even attempted to efface all title to the divine image from their minds."[3] Works on Wilberforce have emphasized that abolition was a religious and humanitarian triumph over economic and political interests.

While humanitarian considerations have received considerable attention, what have been perceived as underlying economic motives continue to be argued passionately. Although the argument for economic factors was championed by the late West Indian historian and politician Eric Williams, this view had intellectual precedents.[4] According to earlier interpretations, the abolition of the slave trade was preceded by a decline in its value to the British economy and a halt in the expansion of the British West Indian colonies. What has become popularly known as the Williams thesis has followed this interpretation.

According to Williams,

> the capitalists had first encouraged West Indian slavery and then helped to destroy it. . . . When British capitalism found the West Indian monopoly a nuisance, they destroyed West Indian slavery as the first step in the destruction of the West Indian monopoly.[5]

Williams distinguished three steps by which mature capitalism destroyed the mercantilist economic system of which slavery formed a part:

> . . . the attack falls into three phases: the attack on the slave trade, the attack on slavery, the attack on the preferential sugar duties. The slave trade was abolished in 1807, slavery in 1833, the sugar preference in 1846. The three events are inseparable. The very vested interests which had been built up by the slave system now turned and destroyed the system. . . . The rise and fall of mercantilism is the rise and fall of slavery.[6]

In spite of the Williams thesis, present research and available evidence indicate that the West Indies were not entering a period of decline during the period of abolition but were profitable and growing.[7] Trade figures do not support a premise of stagnation in the British West Indies. By 1821, West Indian imports and exports were greater than they had been some fifty years earlier.[8] The value of land in the Indies was also rising. While the West Indian planters valued their plantations at £50-60 million in 1775, they were being estimated at £85-100 million in 1807. The inflation factor during this period was negligible. Again, both the capital value and the British overseas trade were expanding rather than declining. British exports to Africa held firm after 1783 in relation to the period before 1775. Furthermore, the British trade in slaves was increasing during the last decades of the eighteenth century when English abolitionists were launching their attack. Not only were British slave-traders doing well between 1750 and 1807 but the British share of the trade also went up.[9] In 1797 one out of every four ships from Liverpool — which since the mid-eighteenth century had taken over from Bristol as the leading English slaving port — was a slaver, with local merchants handling five-eighths of the English trade and three-sevenths of the trade of all Europe; by 1800 they had nine-tenths of the combined trade of England and the rest of Europe. Profits in the British slave trade between 1761 and 1806 were about 10 per cent of the capital invested and were particularly remunerative between 1781 and 1800. Thus the major attack on the slave trade during the first decades of the eighteenth century came at a time and place where the trade was most profitable.

Although one may dispute the details of Williams's thesis, the economic underpinnings that made the abolition of the slave trade possible cannot be denied. Abolition did come at a juncture when material and technological advances were promoting complex economic, social, political and cultural changes. Industrialization and the industrial revolution had economic consequences which shifted the movement of labour and resources from agriculture to industry. Many slave societies, except for those in Cuba and Brazil, where the production of sugar and coffee was still expanding, were reaching a point where the slave population could reproduce itself and adequately meet the labour needs required of it. The period of mercantilist economy was also giving way to a *laissez-faire* situation, and economic thinkers like Adam Smith were arguing that slave labour was manifestly inefficient. In Great Britain, which was the largest slave-trading nation, the new order of industry and commerce was also beginning to overshadow the interest of West Indian slave-owners, who had once been a powerful group in Parliament.

Recent works have shifted attention from a single causal effect to a study of the complex forces that shaped the movement for the abolition of the slave trade and the emancipation of slaves. Those who were in the forefront of this movement shared a common ideology that David B. Davis has defined as "an integrated system of beliefs, assumptions and values, not necessarily true or false, which reflects the needs and interests of a group or class at a particular time in history".[10] Among the groups that came to believe that slavery threatened the destiny of society were Evangelicals, philosophers of enlightenment and revolutionaries of the period.

Anti-slavery ideology emerged in the late eighteenth century after the public had long ignored the evil and horrors of the slave trade. Before this, very few had doubted the justice of the trade, and "good" Christians had simply urged masters to treat their slaves with charity and forbearance. Social change, however, gave rise to newer classes who were receptive to ideas resulting from the convergence of religious, intellectual and literary trends of the period.

What happened to change peoples' views and perceptions of morality and virtue? The Evangelicals, who arose out of the revivalist movements in British and North America, played a role. They believed in the forgiveness of sin and felt summoned by God to make the world righteous, to relieve suffering and prepare the way for the salvation of souls. They thought that slavery was evil and that those enslaved should be redeemed from physical bondage. By 1774, people like John Wesley, the founder of Methodism, had been converted to the anti-slavery movement and saw slavery as a great sin and a stain upon society that had to be removed. The Evangelicals believed that the slave was capable of receiving the great benefits of Christian virtue and hope. The Quakers, who arose out of British Protestantism, were also committed to anti-slavery ideas and shared certain beliefs that, in the late eighteenth century, coincided with the ideas of the anti-slavery.

The rise of secular social philosophy and the ideas emanating from the Enlightenment brought about changes in the manner in which people viewed the slave trade. As more emphasis was given to liberty and happiness, it became evident that slavery was inconsistent with the moral and providential order and should be condemned. The anti-slavery implications of the "noble savages" gave new awareness to the problem, and by the end of the eighteenth century there was little intellectual defence for slavery. These developments led to the popularization of what Professor Davis has called the ethic of benevolence.

While the forces arising out of the ideology of the period spearheaded the anti-slavery movement, the part played by the slaves themselves in effecting the end of the trade should be recognized.[11] Although slave revolts and rebellions in the Americas date from the early sixteenth century, the rebellion that probably had the greatest impact on the slave trade was the one that took place in St Domingue in 1791.

By the mid-eighteenth century, St Domingue had become the most prosperous island of the Caribbean, growing sugar, coffee, indigo, cocoa and cotton. The population of the island consisted of whites, their mulatto descendants and Blacks. Over two-thirds of the island slaves were African born, and culturally many of them were close to their African origins. The islands were divided according to colour and privilege, and the events of the French Revolution of 1789 had a tremendous impact on the whole black population. The principles of the revolution were interpreted in different ways by the residents of the island. Whites, who believed that the power of government had now devolved to them, were divided between royalist and revolutionary opinion. Mulattos viewed the revolution as an opportunity to gain equality with whites, and Blacks hoped it signalled the end of slavery. At the same time, the Revolutionary Assembly in France could not decide whether the principles of the revolution applied to the French colony. Although mulattos were eventually accorded equality with whites, it took an outright revolution to bring about freedom for black slaves.

The incitement for the rebellion came from a slave priest named Boukman in August 1791, when he was presiding over a ritual service. Boukman suggested that Blacks should be paid for their work and that in the future they should be given three days of rest a week. The black slaves present vowed to carry out all of Boukman's suggestions and on 22 August 1791 they agreed to kill all the whites they could find. Some two thousand whites were massacred. The French army responded with serious reprisals, and many slaves, including Boukman, were burned or tortured to death. Nevertheless the Assembly in Paris emancipated the slaves in St Domingue on 4 February 1794.

The slave revolt in St Domingue in a sense became a revolution that affected the course of abolition and emancipation, breeding fear among slave holders, encouraging slaves to rebel and strengthening the anti-slavery movement. Toussaint L'Ouverture, who became leader in St Domingue following the revolt, claimed the same liberty and equality for black slaves that the French were claiming for themselves. Gabriel Prosser's revolt in 1800 in Virginia and Denmark Vesey's rebellion in 1822 in South Carolina all looked to him and to St Domingue for precedent. While the St Domingue slave rebellion and other revolts called attention to the problem of slavery, much of the momentum for change came from the ideological movements of the period.

Abolition in the United States

Abolition had been an important issue in the United States of America long before it emerged elsewhere. As early as 1688, Francis Daniel Pastorius published a petition in Pennsylvania against the slave trade. In the years following this petition, Quakers also made similar protests, but their significant denunciation of the institution did not come until the 1750s, when agitation for abolition increased throughout the United States. In 1754, the Quaker John Woolman published *Considerations on Keeping of Negroes*. Then, in 1775, a group of Quakers organized the first anti-slavery society in America. In 1776 another Quaker, Anthony Benezet, led his group in expelling members of the church who held slaves. The Methodists were also involved in the early anti-slavery movement in America, and in 1784, at the Christmas conference that marked the beginning of American Methodism, John Wesley instituted measures to exclude American slave owners. This stricture was, however, later relaxed to permit Southern slave holders to join the Methodist Church.[12]

Religious agitation against the slave trade coincided with the American Revolution. During the early period of the conflict with

Britain, Quakers pointed out the inconsistency between colonists' demand for freedom and the holding of slaves. They numbered slaveholding among the sins resulting in their suffering during the French and Indian Wars that preceded the revolution. The Quakers helped to popularize voluntary emancipation as a sign of self-purification.

The existence of slavery in the United States contradicted the principles of the American Revolution, and it was clear at the end of the War of Independence that slavery would pose challenging problems to the new nation. The American Revolution, to be sure, did not solve the problem of slavery, but the language of the leaders of the revolution and their concepts of the rights of a free people in a slave-owning society presented an ironic situation. Thus, the ideologies that condemned British tyranny and defended American rights also indicted slavery. Nevertheless, slavery was central to the United States economy at the time of the War of Independence. Since the war had been fought over the issue of self-determination, most American leaders were aware of the obstacles to be met in abolishing slavery. The constitutional convention of 1787 thus resolved the question of the slave trade by deferring abolition.

According to Article 1, Section 9, of the United States Constitution: "The Migration or importation of such persons as any of the States now existing shall think proper to admit, shall not be prohibited by the Congress prior to the year one thousand eight hundred and eight, but a tax or duty may be imposed on such Importation, not exceeding ten dollars for each Person." The Constitution gave Congress the power and authority to regulate commerce among the several states and foreign nations and thus the authority to regulate the slave trade. Although various states tried to pass laws dealing with abolition, it was Congress that finally initiated a binding law to end the trade. On 2 March 1807, President Jefferson signed "An Act to prohibit the importation of slaves into any port or place within the jurisdiction of the United States, from and after the first day of January, in the year of Our Lord one thousand eight hundred and eight".

England and abolition

In 1765 in England, the public fight against the slave trade was begun by Granville Sharp, a government employee at the Ordinance Office. Sharp and his brother William, who was a medical doctor, aided a slave, one Jonathan Strong, who had been savagely beaten by his master. Sharp was able to free Strong and prevent his master from sending him back to the West Indies. Indeed, the number of Blacks in Britain had grown larger, with West Indian planters bringing slaves into the country as domestic servants.[13] The issues raised in the case of Strong climaxed with the famous case of James Somerset in 1772, in which Justice Mansfield ruled that the master had no right forcibly to remove his slave from England. According to Lord Mansfield, "The State of Slavery is so odious that nothing can be suffered to support it but positive law. Whatever inconvenience may follow the decision, I cannot say that the case is allowed or approved by the Law of England, and therefore the black must be discharged".[14] Although the judgment called attention to their plight, Mansfield's decision did not free black slaves in England and there was nothing in his ruling to indicate that "as soon as any slave set foot on English ground he becomes free".[15]

In 1779 Granville Sharp continued his fight against the slave trade by getting the issue of slavery raised in the House of Commons. He hoped by this to call greater attention to the inequities of the trade in order to get it stopped. In 1783, Sharp unsuccessfully attempted to prosecute the people responsible for throwing slaves overboard from the slave ship Zong. In 1787, when the Abolition Committee was formed, Sharp agreed to serve as Chairman because the Committee felt that his name and influence would aid them in their work.

The work of the Abolition Committee contributed to the ending of the slave trade. The abolition movement was successful partly because it appealed to people at all levels of society. The people who came together in 1787 to co-ordinate their efforts created popular sentiment for abolition through lectures, distribution of tracts and newspaper articles. The judicial decisions of the 1770s had created a more favourable political climate for the movement. The increase in the black population in London in the 1760s (to about 20,000), the increase in the population of black refugees in the United States after 1783, the founding of a committee "for the

Relief of the Black Poor" in England and the establishment of a settlement in Sierra Leone in 1787 as a home for free Blacks — all called attention to the problem of slavery. The London Committee stated:

> Our immediate aim is, by diffusing a knowledge of the subject, and particularly the Modes of procuring and treating slaves, to interest men of every description in the Abolition of the Traffick; but especially those from whom any alteration must proceed — the Members of our Legislature.[16]

Thomas Clarkson became a leading member of the committee on abolition. A graduate of Cambridge University, he had won an essay prize on the subject: "Is it right to make slaves of others against their will?" Between 1787 and 1794 he travelled some 35,000 miles within Great Britain; his journeys as well as his writings against the slave trade were of great significance, and Clarkson helped establish local committees for abolition and sought support among people of note who would be sympathetic to abolition. He became acquainted with William Wilberforce, who led the fight against the slave trade in Parliament. As a boy of fourteen years, Wilberforce had written to a newspaper in York to condemn the slave trade and for him the cause of abolition had become a sacred charge.

By 1788, Parliament was being inundated the petitions from abolition committees to end the slave trade. In February of that year, William Willberforce and William Pitt, the Prime Minister who sympathized with the abolitionist cause, decided that factual information which would discredit the slave trade must be assembled before abolition could take place. Pitt chose a committee of the Privy Council to investigate, but it was not until April 1789 that the committee made its report. Thus, there were no factual bases for debating the slave-trade issue in 1788, as Pitt had hoped.

The abolitionists, however, won one important victory in the Slave Trade Regulating Act of 1788, which was also known as the Dolben's Act. This bill placed a limit on the number of slaves that could be carried relative to a ship's tonnage. It also offered bounties for slave captains and surgeons bringing slaves to their destinations alive. Even before this act was passed, William Pitt introduced a motion on 9 May 1788 that during the next session, the House would "take into consideration the circumstances of the slave trade".[17] Following the publication of the Report of the Privy Council Committee, Wilberforce on 12 May 1789 introduced a motion in Parliament for the abolition of the slave trade.

Despite the information provided by the Report of the Privy Council, the members of Parliament demanded to conduct their own hearing. An Abstract of the Evidence was produced in 1790 by a Parliamentary Committee, and in April 1791 another motion for abolition was introduced, only to be voted down. Following this defeat, it became ncessary for abolitionists to reach beyond Parliament and appeal to the justice and humanity of Great Britain as a nation. The effort to reach the people and disseminate information about the slave trade led to petitions from abolitionists to Parliament, and the more radical abolitionists renounced the use of sugar during this period. However, in spite of bills which abolitionist interests sponsored in Parliament to abolish the trade little had been accomplished by 1804.[18]

Although the political climate from 1804 onwards was more favourable towards ending the slave trade, abolition bills introduced in 1804 and 1805 failed to be passed, despite great exertions on the part of their supporters. By the end of 1805, after appealing to national interests, abolitionists managed to get British slavers to stop the supply of slaves to French colonies conquered by the British during the Napoleonic Wars.

Support for abolition in 1806 appeared to be growing. Instead of having Wilberforce introduce another bill for a blanket abolition of the slave trade, abolitionists first initiated a measure that would end the supply of slaves to the conquered islands and to foreign colonies. After a bill passed in May 1806 in effect halted nearly two-thirds of the British trade, the abolitionists tried to get the whole trade abolished. To this end, a bill was introduced in Parliament on 10 June 1806, resolving:

> That this House, considering the African slave trade to be contrary to the principles of justice, humanity, and sound policy, will, with all practicable expedition take effectual measure for the abolition of the said trade, in such manner, and at such period, as may be deemed advisable.[19]

The Abolition Bill finally passed both Houses of Parliament, received the royal assent on 25 March 1807 and became effective on 1 May 1807. Roger Anstey says:

> The key to the eventual passage of abolition is the way in which the abolitionists conceived the tactic of so using a particular, fortuitous conjunction in Britain's politico-economic position, brought about by war as to present the abolition of up to two-thirds of the British slave trade as an elementary dictate of the national interest in time of War.[20]

Complying with abolition

Great Britain used stringent legislation to ensure that her own subjects would abandon the trade. The Act of Parliament which abolished the slave trade called for the forfeiture of British ships engaged in the trade, as well as a fine of £100 for every slave impounded. In 1811, still pressing compliance with the abolition act, Britain declared the participation in slave trade a felony punishable by transportation to penal colonies, and also made strenuous efforts to enlist other nations in the abolition movement. This task fell upon the British Navy and Foreign Office. The Foreign Office conducted the negotiations, and the Navy attempted to enforce the agreements on the high seas.[21] Denmark abolished the slave trade in 1802, Sweden in 1813, Holland in 1814 and France in 1815.[22]

When the Treaty of Ghent was signed at the end of the Anglo-American war of 1812, Britain and America agreed to strive to suppress the trade on a world-wide basis. At the Congress of Vienna following the Napoleonic Wars, Lord Castlereagh proposed an international police force to help suppress the trade. When the proposal failed, it became the responsibility of Great Britain to establish the necessary force.

While Great Britain was essentially interested in international agreements to stop the trade, she made bilateral agreements with various nations,[23] including Portugal, Brazil and Spain. To get Portugal and Spain to comply, England had to resort to payments and by 1853 had paid sums amounting to about £3,000,000 to Portugal and £1,000,000 to Spain. In 1816, Britain concluded a treaty with Portugal, who agreed to abolish the trade north of the Equator. Portugal also agreed to allow the British navy to search her vessels for illicit slave cargo north of the line.

In 1814, Spain agreed to proscribe the trade except for supplying slaves to her possessions. In 1817 she agreed to stop trading slaves north of the Equator, and in 1820 she agreed to abolish the trade entirely. The treaty of 1817 gave Britain the right to detain Spanish ships with slaves on board who had been taken from African territory north of the Equator. The treaty also provided for the establishment of Courts of Mixed Commissions, made up of the principal nations seeking to abolish the trade and the nations participating illegally in it, in order to adjudicate disputes and try ship captains violating the treaty.[24]

The right to search ships to determine if they were carrying slaves was an important step, and such agreements were obtained between 1817 and 1841 with many nations. However, tighter controls were needed since captains, even though their ships were obviously in Africa to trade in slaves, could not be condemned if they were not caught with captives aboard. Thus, England pressed for what became known as Equipment Treaties.[25] Under these pacts, ships found containing shackles, bolts, handcuffs and excessive quantities of water and food could be impounded.

In 1817, a Court of Mixed Commission was set up at Sierra Leone to adjudicate matters concerning ships seized by British cruisers. In addition, there were courts in St Helena, Barbados, the Cape, Luanda, Rio de Janeiro, Surinam, Havana and New York. Many of the activities of the Courts of Mixed Commission took place in Sierra Leone, since the Navy concentrated on intercepting ships at the points of embarkation rather than disembarkation. Thus, Courts of Mixed Commission at arrival points such as Havana and Rio declined in importance.

Spain and Brazil offered the most resistance to the abolition of the slave trade because they still needed slaves in Cuba and Brazil.[26] Cuba was an important trading partner to Spain during this period and Cuban revenues provided funds for the Carlist Wars of the 1830s. So important was Cuba to Spain that one Captain General of the island pointed out that it represented more to modern Spain than all the American continent represented to their ancestors. Thus British abolitionist campaigns threatened Spanish colonial policy in an area Spain regarded as vital to her New World interest and so Spain resisted British efforts. In 1826, Brazil made a commitment stipulating that, after 1830, trading in slaves would be considered equivalent to piracy and passed laws in 1831 providing for severe penalties for slave trading. These laws were not enforced and were replaced by milder provisions that permitted captured slaves to be auctioned in the Rio market to people paying the highest yearly "rent" for them.

The trade continued with the full knowledge and approval of the Brazilian government. Between 1849-50, the British intensified action to stop the slave merchants, and her threat of blockading the country's ports led Brazil to take action to end the slave trade in 1852.[27]

In spite of earlier agreements with Spain, the slave trade to Cuba continued. Spain was highly reluctant to bow to Great Britain's orders when Britain threatened unilateral action to stop the trade. In Cuba, opinion regarding slavery pitted the planters and merchants against the intellectual community, which deprecated the continuance of the slave trade and felt that the institution of slavery would crumble once the trade ended. Others thought that slavery was uneconomic and should be replaced by a paid labour system. By the 1830s there were reformers in Cuba who wanted to maintain slavery while abolishing the slave trade. There were also racially conscious Whites who viewed the presence of a large number of Blacks in Cuba and in the neighbouring Caribbean islands as a physical threat and supported abolition for this reason.[28]

By the 1860s, many wealthy planters were openly seeking gradual abolition with compensation for slave owners. In 1865, an anti-slave trade association was formed in Cuba, strongly espousing abolition with compensation. Spain was too poor to pay compensation. Before any substantive action on the slave trade could be taken, however, a civil war (1868-78) broke out in Cuba which contributed to the driving of Isabella II from the Spanish throne in 1869.[29]

Slavery became an important issue during the Ten Years War. On 4 July 1870, Spain passed the Moret Law which granted freedom to every child born after that date. The statute also made slaves born between 17 September 1868 and 4 July 1870 property of the state and paid their masters 125 Spanish pesetas per person.

Slaves who had served under the Spanish flag, who had performed valuable services, who were over 60 years of age or who belonged to the state, as well as those who wanted to return to Africa, were freed.[30]

Despite strong resistance, emancipation continued in Cuba, and in fact the slave population had been gradually decreasing from the middle of the nineteenth century. From 1869 to 1878, the slave population fell from 363,000 to about 228,000 — a decline of 37 per cent. During the five-year period from 1870 to 1875, the Moret Law affected 64 per cent of the slaves who gained their freedom. In 1879, the Spanish government issued a new emancipation law that went into effect on 29 July 1880.[31] By 1888, slavery and the slave trade were virtually dead in Cuba.

In addition to its efforts to suppress the trade through diplomacy within Europe, Great Britain negotiated with African chiefs to sign treaties encouraging them to refrain from participating in the slave trade, and between 1842 and 1850 over forty such treaties were signed. In 1841, King Pepple of Bonny (on the coast of modern Nigeria) signed a treaty with Britain which would give him goods up to the value of £500 every year for five years in exchange for giving up the slave trade. Many African leaders, however, found it difficult to honour the treaties because the legitimate trade in which they were encouraged to participate yielded fewer dividends than the slave trade.[32]

Emancipation in the British colonies

The years immediately following the British abolition of the slave trade saw little activity against slavery within the colonies; however, by 1822 concern had re-emerged.[33] James Cropper, a Liverpool Quaker, was an important figure in the anti-slavery effort. Having been involved in the earlier activities against the trade, he now wanted action against slavery. In 1822 the ageing William Wilberforce, who had led the abolitionists' fight in Parliament, handed over the leadership of the abolitionist movement to T.R. Buxton. In May 1823, Buxton introduced a bill in Parliament for the gradual abolition of slavery in Britain's colonies. The bill failed, and for the next ten years there was little action because of the large West Indian interests of those in Parliament who were against emancipation of slaves. As for grassroots pressure, while the British public was aware of the evils of the slave trade they were unfamiliar with the grim realities of a plantation slave's existence.

However, in the 1830s, missionaries, free mulattos and slaves in the British colonies brought considerable pressure on local legislatures. During this period, slaves became increasingly restive, and violent outbreaks occurred in Guiana, Barbados and Jamaica. In many of these instances, slaves had in fact heard of discussions in Britain about possible emancipation. At Le Resouvenir in Guiana, in 1823, slaves demanded immediate emancipation and killed their masters when they resisted. In Jamaica in 1831, slaves, believing that emancipation had already been granted but was being withheld, began to riot.

Although all these activities influenced public opinion, it was the support which the anti-slavery forces received from the Parliament that convened in 1833 that made the bill abolishing slavery a reality. The Emancipation Act became law in August that year, decreeing "that slavery shall be abolished throughout the British Colonies, on, from and after the First of August, 1834". Nevertheless, the slaves did not immediately gain absolute freedom, since a transitional period of six years' "apprenticeship" was provided for, during which time they were to continue working as unpaid servants for three-quarters of the week (while being permitted to hire out their services for the remainder of the week, although they could buy their freedom if they could meet the stipulated price). Eventually the period of apprenticeship was shortened throughout the colonies, and on 1 August 1838 the ex-slaves were at last fully free.

Emancipation in the United States

Between 1807, when the slave trade was outlawed by Parliament, and 1831, the year of a major slave revolt in the southern United States, objections were increasingly raised against slavery. Anti-slavery initiatives were in some ways more effective in the South than they were in the North. In 1817 the American Colonization Society — incorporated under the name "The American Society for Colonizing the Free People of Color of the United States" — was founded, including southern leaders like Chief Justice John Marshall, President James Monroe and the famous senator from Kentucky, Henry Clay.[34] The Society raised funds to remunerate slave owners, and freed slaves were sent back to Africa, where in 1822 the first colonists founded Liberia (whose capital, Monrovia, was named after the American president). The movement initially received good response in the South, and at one time there were 200 groups, with certain churches and ministers playing a prominent role in the organization. It failed in the long run probably because a number of black and white abolitionists campaigned against the society, since it masked racist and pro-slavery sentiment, incorporating members who hoped to increase the value of their own slaves by ridding themselves of troublesome free Blacks, as well as members who simply wanted to be relieved of all responsibility for the rights of free Blacks. In spite of all this, by 1860 an estimated 4,000 slaves had been sent to Liberia.

The writings of William Lloyd Garrison were especially important in shaping public opinion in the United States. He was converted to the anti-slavery cause by Benjamin Lundy, a New Jersey Quaker, and in January 1831 began publishing the *Public Liberator and Journal of the Times*, where he unequivocally stated his attitude towards slavery:

> I will be as harsh as truth, and as uncompromising as justice. On this subject I do not wish to think, speak, or write, with moderation. No! Tell a man whose house is on fire to give a moderate alarm; tell him to moderately rescue his wife from the hands of a ravisher; tell the mother to gradually extricate her babe from the fire into which it has fallen — but urge me not to use moderation in a cause like the present. I am in earnest — I will not equivocate — I will not retreat a single inch — and I will be heard!

He demanded immediate abolition, and although his impact on the movement may be debated, his actions heightened Southern opposition to slavery. In 1833, following the abolition of slavery in the British colonies, the American Anti-Slavery Society was formed. This group became very influential through lectures, conferences and the distribution of literature, and by 1840 had made abolition a national crusade.[35] This crusade embodied both moral and political anti-slavery feelings. Political anti-slavery contributed much to the sectional conflict leading to the Civil War.

While the anti-slavery movement was gaining momentum, events in the South were calling attention to the dangers presented by black slaves. In August 1831, Nat Turner, a black slave preacher of Southampton County in Virginia, and a band of followers killed 61 Whites. This incident inspired terror among white Southerners; following the rebellion, advocates of emancipation were no longer welcomed in the South and many of them were either silenced or moved north. The Nat Turner rebellion aroused anger in the South that was focused on the new emancipation movement, and Southern spokesmen began to defend their institution aggressively. Scripture and history were quoted to support slavery as a positive good. Some tried to use "scientific" evidence to show that black men were inferior. Slave codes were instituted to regulate the conduct and movement of slaves. They were forbidden to leave their plantations without a permit, forbidden to own firearms, to visit free Negroes or to assemble unless Whites were present. The problem of slavery was also injected into the religious and the political life of the American nation. The slave issue forced Presbyterians and Baptists to divide into northern and southern factions. The sectional conflict between the North and the South reached its final extreme with the outbreak of the Civil War in 1861, resulting in the emancipation of the slaves in 1863.

Brazil and emancipation

Brazil did not go through the wrenching experience of a civil war in order to abolish slavery. Given the importance of the institution to the Brazilian economy, however, the attempt to end the trade was not easy. Even after the "Declaration of the Rights of Man" in the Brazilian Constitution of 1824, freedom for slaves remained distant. But with the abolition of the trade in 1852, slavery in Brazil was doomed to eventual extinction. The anti-slavery movement that emerged in Brazil in the 1860s was weak and drew much of its inspiration from abroad. Nevertheless, the decade culminated in legislation, ratified in 1871, that freed all children born of slave parents.

Those who came to favour abolition were people committed to justice and social change as well as those who accepted emancipation because it was unavoidable. Social groups least tied to slavery, such as professionals and government functionaries, supported abolition. Urban classes, both native and foreign born, who found new opportunities for work in an urban setting also lent their support.

The movement intensified in the 1880s. By then, with slave escapes, revolts and increased tensions about the destiny of slavery, it seemed that a social revolution was imminent. There was a clear split between representatives from the north-eastern provinces, who agreed to the discussion of slavery in Parliament, and those from coffee-growing regions, who wanted to maintain the status quo. Campaign speeches, public meetings and the activities of groups which aided escaped slaves increased. In this atmosphere, emancipation proceeded quickly in those provinces least tied to slavery. In 1884, slavery was abolished in Amazonias and Ceara. In spite of continued defence of the institution, especially from the sugar-growing regions of Campos and coffee-growing areas of Rio de Janeiro and São Paulo, slavery seemed doomed and disintegrated quickly after 1884. This process was aided by the mass escape of slaves. The army, whose duty it was to catch and return the runaways to their owners, closed their eyes to the flight of fugitives. In these circumstances, owners, unable to prevent the escape of their slaves, preferred to free them on condition that they would work for them. Reluctantly, slave owners came to accept the situation. Thus, it was not surprising that, in 1867, the Republican Party, made up largely of coffee-plantation owners in São Paulo, approved an agreement that they should free their slaves by 14 July 1889. With Brazil facing *de facto* abolition, the chamber of deputies abolished slavery on 13 May 1888.

The abolition of slavery in Brazil in 1888 climaxed efforts that had begun in the last quarter of the eighteenth century. The ideology that characterized the abolition movement operated within certain shared notions and beliefs that were characteristic of the Western European nations and the colonies they established in the New World. The notions that shaped the attitude of Western Europeans and their slave colonies in the Americas emanated from biblical and historical beliefs which gave substance to an ideological movement with an evangelical and philosophical base that was concerned with reform. The interest in reform, however, was not a narrow concern for slaves as such. Nor was the fight for abolition and emancipation an admission that black people were equal to whites. Very few of the people who championed the cause of abolition could in fact have looked at the symbol of the British abolition movement — the kneeling, manacled black, asking: "Am I not a man and a brother?" — and answered the question with an unqualified yes. The important consideration was that the abolition movement ended the slave trade and slavery in the Americas. Yet the grim institutions that had existed for so long were not without impact upon the societies that were involved with them.

6
The Legacy of the Slave Trade in Africa

The impact of the West on Africa is often perceived as the interaction between a dynamic Western society and a passive African one. This is especially true of discussions about the consequences of the slave trade for Africa. This preconception implies ignorance of indigenous African cultures, as well as of the fact that the consequences of the trade went beyond the moral and ethical ones. As horrible and morally repugnant as the trade was, it did not break the spirit, initiative or resilience of the African societies which suffered the rape of their human resources, although to affirm this adaptability does not deny the baneful implications of a trade that removed millions of Africans who were at the most productive period of their lives. The negative impact of removing so many people from any society cannot be denied, especially when labour is exported in return for finished goods. The very manner of acquiring slaves in Africa did not help provide the necessary economic base for future development.

The victims of the slave trade were obtained through warfare, trickery and banditry. Undeniably the destructive impact of the slave trade upon African society made any advance and development difficult. According to the historian Walter Rodney:

> The European slave trade was a direct block in removing millions of youths and young adults who are the human agents from whom inventiveness springs. Those who remained in areas regularly affected by slave-capturing were more preoccupied with their freedom than with improvements in production. Besides, even the busiest African in West, Central or East Africa was concerned more with trade than with production, because of the nature of the contacts with Europe; and that situation was not conducive to the introduction of technological advances.[1]

Normal economic activities could not be pursued alongside the slave trade, for it was difficult to procure both slaves and ordinary trade goods from the same area — the slave trade sublimated customary exchanges. Furthermore, African rulers and a few other principal persons established the demand for imports, and favoured consumption goods and luxuries that did little to create new wealth. The threat of enslavement increased fear and insecurity and stifled the creativity which might have led to improvements in Africa. People preoccupied with their safety and security have little incentive to attempt qualitative and quantitative advances in their society. As the Nigerian historian G.N. Uzoigwe states: "the uncertainty and fear created in the areas thus affected made any economic development impossible. Industries, where they once existed, no longer flourished. This was particularly true of the African metallurgical and textile industries of West Africa which were ruined partly by the slave trade."[2]

Clearly, the conflict between a trade that exported labour and an economy wherein most production was labour-intensive was insurmountable. To comprehend the impact of the slave trade upon Africa, we need to understand the changes that the trade brought to African society. But evaluating this is difficult, not only because of the complexities involved but because the slave trade did not become the dominant export on the African coast until the eighteenth century. In order to arrive at a balanced view of the changes brought by the slave trade, it may help to look at African societies in terms of categories similar to those employed earlier.

Demography

During the years of the slave trade, the continent remained relatively inaccessible. Penetration of the African interior was difficult, and the manner of travel and transportation changed very little. Except for the Kongo-Angola area, Europeans were confined to the coastal areas and had to deal with African middlemen. To facilitate trade with the interior, a number of small villages evolved into important commercial centres that later became bridgeheads for the penetration of Africa by the Portuguese, Dutch, British, Danish, French and Swedish.

On the Gold Coast, because of intense competition between European traders, urban centres evolved around several dozen European forts and settlements along the coast, such as at Elmina,

Dixcove, Cape Coast, Cormantine, Shama and Christiansborg, among many others. The presence of these urban centres led to the rise of a group of Africans and Afro-Europeans who, as agents for the trade, were closely tied to a European society whose values and ideas lay beyond those of traditional Africa. The emergence of urban areas reflected the movement of populations. This raises the question of the slave trade's impact on population.

The population of Africa declined as a result of the slave trade. There were those who died in wars and raids, others during the march to the coast and some died while waiting for the slave ships to arrive. This loss of people was associated with the disruption of life in Africa.

The loss of people through the slave trade invariably affected agricultural development on the continent. As the work of Ester Boserup has demonstrated, population growth can be a major factor in determining agricultural developments, and can result in frequent cropping and technological changes to help with the production and yield of crops. Thus population growth, the intensive use of the land and the need to increase production often lead to the invention of better tools, which in turn allow the output per man-hour in food production to increase and permit part of the population to engage in non-agricultural activities. Because of the slave trade, however, the population in Africa was not allowed to reach the point where it could have made this breakthrough.[3] Although the population did decline, it is also possible that there was a decline in mortality in this era, due to the introduction of certain food crops such as maize, corn, peanuts and plantains, which became the staple foods in many areas affected by the slave trade.[4] Since the ratio of export was two men for every woman, it is also probable that some of the loss of population was made up through the institutions such as polygamy.

The impact of the trade on various regions differed over time and place. No coastal region experienced constant high export throughout the entire period of the slave trade. Senegambia, one of the earliest areas to be exploited, furnished about a third of the slaves for the Atlantic trade prior to the sixteenth century. In terms of the absolute number of exports, the peak of the trade was not reached until about 1710, but this time slaves were being brought through

Senegambia, not originating there. Thereafter the Portuguese moved further down the coast, and Senegambia ceased to be a major source of slaves.[5]

Upper Guinea accounted for about one-third of the slaves exported during the early phase when the Portuguese dominated the commerce. The area of modern Sierra Leone also contributed large numbers for a short time in the mid-sixteenth century. The invasion of Sierra Leone by the people known as the Mane and the conflict that it generated produced slaves until the early part of the seventeenth century. Although exports from the region ceased to be important after this period, there were spurts of exports from the region in the 1720s and 1740s which were associated with the Fulbe *jihads* (holy wars) in the Fuuta Jaalon area.[6]

The expanded export of slaves from the Gold Coast through the 1740s coincided with the rise, expansion and consolidation of the Asante empire. Exports from the 1750s cannot be correlated with any particular period of war, and probably reflect tribute payments in slave exports that the Asante received from their conquered subjects.[7]

On the Windward Coast, which includes the modern area of Liberia, the increase in slave exports from the 1720s through the 1740s was linked with the Islamic holy war in Fuuta Jaalon in the 1720s and the expansion of the Kuranko tribe into the upper part of Guinea-Conakry.[8] A second increase in the 1770s was associated with the westward expansion of the Asante. Similarly the peak of exports in the Bight of Benin related to political change in the area. The peak around 1710 was based on exports from Whydah and was reached before Dahomey conquered the area in the 1720s. The other peak in the 1780s was associated with slaves brought from Oyo at a period when the Oyo ruler Alafin Abiodun (c. 1770-89) increased the slave trade of Oyo.[9]

The Bight of Biafra was a negligible supplier of slaves until the 1730s, when political and structural changes and the spread and control of interior trading networks increased the slave imports. Efficient organization and gathering of slaves through trading networks allowed the people of the Bight of Biafra to export large numbers of slaves without resorting to large-scale warfare.[10] The Kongo-Angola area consistently supplied slaves throughout the period of trade but the area of provenance changed over time, until traders reached deep into the farthest interior.[11]

Recent research on the trade in the Bight of Benin has revealed a large export of the Aja peoples at an annual average of 8,500 between 1690 and 1740.[12] The cumulative total over a fifty-year period has been estimated to be about 3 per cent of their average year-to-year population — a figure that could not have been offset by births. The rate of Aja slave exports for the rest of the eighteenth century averaged between 1 per cent to 2 per cent of their total population, which was still high. The Bariba and the Yoruba were also involved in the slave exports. When all factors are taken into consideration, the population export for the Bight of Benin during the nineteenth century as a whole was 1 per cent per year of the total population. Since most of the slaves came from within 200 kilometres of the coast, the Bight of Benin bore the brunt of the dislocation caused by the trade in that region.

Again, the Eastern region of the Gold Coast, about 80 to 100 miles inland north of Accra (the capital of modern Ghana), saw a considerable decline in population. Although figures are not available, when the trade ended in this area, which included the eastern part of the Akyem state, the westernmost areas of Akuapem, Akwamu and Accra were largely empty.[13] Other regions of the country do not seem to have been similarly denuded of population. According to a recent study, the population of Angola also fell during the slave trade, notwithstanding a Portuguese census that claimed that the population was held in balance through natural increase.[14]

The period also saw a movement of people to the coastal enclaves where centres emerged to handle the trade between Africa and Europe. Beyond the demographic impact of the trade, however, there were also economic changes that any trading relationship brings about.

Economic impact

Whatever the morality of their actions, the African slave-traders who dealt with Europeans during four centuries of the trade demonstrated that they were merchants of acumen. They organized a far-flung commercial network that delivered many millions of their fellow countrymen into slavery. It is sometimes asserted that the goods that Africans accepted in return for their slaves were essentially rubbish or goods of very poor quality. Although these men may have been greedy or short-sighted in selling the best asset of their country, they cannot be accused of stupidity. In fact, Africans met European traders on the coast on equal terms and could accept or reject the commercial items that they had to offer. It is known that European traders always chose their trading goods carefully to suit African tastes and interests.

Although the wealth produced by the slave trade was unevenly distributed, African society responded to external contact, despite the deadly effects of slaving. The availability of some products offered in exchange for slaves, notably textiles, iron, guns and liquor, has been blamed for forestalling their manufacture within Africa. The finished goods that Africans received were consumption-oriented and in many cases discouraged diversification and structural change in the economy, but there were areas where African production continued during and after the slave trade. Research by Marion Johnson indicates that, although the impact of European imports differed from area to area, African cotton manufacture, for example, did not decline severely.[15] Generally, however, most African industries were of the cottage type and it is difficult to assess the impact of foreign supplies on such manufacturing. In lower Senegal the main weaving industry located up-river continued to function throughout the slave trade era, and in fact the area is still known for its weaving and dyeing. Weaving also flourished in Gambia and Sierra Leone during and after the slave trade ceased.

The import of iron was not necessarily destructive to African metallurgy and its increased availability may have stimulated tool-making. Africans never attempted to manufacture guns in quantity because of the cost involved; African smiths, nevertheless, were skilled in the repair of guns.[16] A contemporary observer wrote that Africans on the Gold Coast were able to turn "old guns sold to them that would not fire to such perfection as scarcely ever to miss".[17] African gunsmiths were also knowledgeable enough about proof-testing to have done their own and then repaired the barrels found to be defective.[18]

The existence of the slave trade has also been blamed for stifling other kinds of trade, but the fact is that staples like gold, ivory and gum were exported continuously by African societies. The recent research of David Northrup shows that the exportation of palm oil from the Niger Delta in the nineteenth century developed before the decline of the slave trade.[19] The slave trade itself generated ancillary economic activities. Slaves marching from the interior and awaiting shipment to the coast had to be fed and the slave ships had to take ample food for their cargo during the middle passage.[20] Activities connected with the transportation, sale, storage of goods and the conduct of the slave trade undoubtedly extended into the interior, just as the slave trade itself did.

To sum up, certain industries continued throughout the period of the slave trade, but although there were increases in the volume of certain trades it was not a period of economic development. In spite of the economic changes, the direct profits from the slave trade went to the chiefs, nobles and merchants involved, and the material gains they received rarely filtered down to the society as a whole.

African politics and changes in community

As with other aspects of the society, discussion of the African political impact of the slave trade has often had a narrow focus. Most accounts feature the link between the exchange of European firearms for slaves and the organization of force to encourage the capture of more slaves in order to trade for more guns, thus maintaining a vicious cycle. According to this interpretation, the slave trade monopoly and importation of guns led to the expansion of the militaristic states involved and the devastation of surrounding regions.

The state of Dahomey is often cited as the classic example of such a society, allegedly maintaining a slave-trade economy through a royal monopoly, exchanging slaves for guns. However, the bulk of recent evidence implies that there is nothing to suggest that Dahomey was so completely subject to the influence of the Atlantic slave trade.[21] The revisionist position shows that a fully developed Dahomey successfully integrated the Atlantic slave trade into its national economy, and it has been estimated that this trade amounted to only 2.5 per cent of the national production of

Dahomey. Furthermore, the socio-economic basis of power, including internal policing of the state, remained unaffected. Guns were not responsible for maintaining the king's power; it was upheld by the traditional structure and the Dahomean system of surveillance and espionage. The internal policies of Dahomey were not determined by the slave trade. Annual wars were influenced not by the trade but by the ideological, political and economic strength of the state. Dahomey was not expanding during the slave-trade era but remained historically stable. Thus, the expansion and centralization of power and authority in Dahomey preceded the gun-slave-gun cycle and was not dependent on a slave-trade economy dominated by a royal monopoly. The state of Dahomey survived the trade and remained viable until it was conquered by the French in 1893.

Other states, admittedly, were not as fortunate. The Kongo was completely devastated by its slave-trading experience. When the Portuguese encountered Kongo in 1482, the kingdom had achieved a degree of centralization and political control. The early contacts between the Europeans and the Africans implied diplomatic parity and there was an early exchange of ambassadors. The ruler of Kongo, Nzinga Nkuwu, requested missionaries and technicians, and went so far as to have his household baptized. The chief's heir, Mbemba Nzinga, or Afonso I, believed in the superiority of the civilization that the Portuguese represented and tried to propagate the Christian religion. The Portuguese, however, did not reciprocate. As Portugal's attention shifted to the East Indies, Kongo became a source of slaves, especially for Portuguese who settled on São Tomé island, off the African coast. The slave trade had started before Afonso I came to power but increased during the four decades he ruled.[22]

During the first two decades of contact with the Portuguese, only 60 slaves were exported from the Kongo. Between 1506 and 1578, however, approximately 345,000 were exported. Even the resident Catholic priests took part in the trade.[23] Although the Portuguese in 1512 had issued a statute (*regimento*) to govern Afro-Portuguese relationships, the master plan for the acculturation of Kongo was subverted by the greed of Portuguese officials, who were more interested in material gain than cultural dissemination.

By 1526, Portuguese preoccupation with the slave trade was

wreaking havoc on the Kongo, and Afonso tried to ban all trade and to expel whites who were not teachers or missionaries. He was forced to revoke the order because many of his chiefs had become involved in the trade, and he wrote in desperation to João of Portugal in 1526:

> There are many traders in all corners of the country. Every day people are enslaved and kidnapped, even nobles, even members of the king's own family.[24]

Afonso I lost half of his kingdom as the Portuguese expanded their trade. Weakened by the impact of the trade, the people of the Kongo were unable to resist the Jaga invasion in 1569, and both the ruler and the Portuguese were thrown out of the country's capital. The destructive effect of the Portuguese slave-traders in Kongo interior was such that, by 1611, the Portuguese Crown banned whites from the interior. The decree had virtually no effect and was later rescinded.

While Dahomey came to terms with slaving and the Kongo was destroyed by the trade, others held back from full participation. Such a state was Benin.[25] As early as 1516, the ruler of Benin began to restrict the export of male slaves; the restriction became a complete embargo towards the late seventeenth century. Although the embargo was lifted in the eighteenth century, the slave trade in this area remained small. From time to time, the ruler of Benin forced Europeans to buy slaves before they were allowed to trade in African-made cotton textiles, beads and ivory. Prices for slaves in Benin were higher than elsewhere on the African coast, and Europeans preferred the cheaper supplies. Even at the peak period of the slave trade in the area, in the late eighteenth century, the yearly exports averaged only a thousand slaves. By the early nineteenth century, Benin was no longer a participant in the slave trade. It would seem that the survival of Benin did not depend upon the slave trade, and it continued as a major state until the late nineteenth century.

The kingdoms of Dahomey, Benin and Kongo are examples of African states that existed prior to the Atlantic slave trade, thus it is incorrect to assert, as has been done, that European contact and trade were in some manner responsible for generating states on the

African coast. The internal history of African states points to the fact that they rose prior to the European presence and, in two of the three cases cited, co-existed with slaving successfully.

While larger political structures were less closely linked with slaving than has been assumed, the slave trade introduced profound changes in the community structure of African society. Among the people of the Niger Delta, kinship as the basis of social organization was replaced by what came to be known as a "House" system. This system of community was based on common economic interests and necessities, rather than on kinship. The House came to incorporate the master, his family and slaves, with each person assigned a rank in the hierarchy, with appropriate duties, responsibilities and privileges. The leader of the House was an absolute ruler with powers of life and death over his domain.[26]

The House, as it evolved in the Niger Delta, became a co-operative trading unit. Smaller Houses ranged from 300 to 1,000 persons, with some large Houses having thousands of slaves, who were used in trade, production and in military roles. Once a member of the House, irrespective of social origin, anyone especially skilled in trade and war could rise to become the Master, as one slave named JaJa did in the nineteenth century.

Beyond the Niger Delta, kinship ties remained the basis of family relationships, and other forms of social structure remained relatively constant. There was, however, one important adaptation. When the slave trade was officially abolished during the nineteenth century, African economic structures that had been adapted to the use of slaves continued to collect them, despite the loss of the external market, and these people had to be incorporated into kinship structures of the society.[27]

Diaspora in reverse

One of the less well known aspects of the slave trade even after its abolition was the return of former slaves from abroad to Africa. In the late eighteenth century Paul Cuffe (1758-1817), a free Black American who had taken his father's first name as a surname, attempted an organized return of Blacks to Africa. A shipbuilder and captain, Cuffe took thirty-eight families to Sierra Leone in

1815 at his own expense. Although his effort ultimately failed, this did not discourage others from making similar attempts at a later date. Africans from the diaspora were also among the people who helped found Liberia and Sierra Leone. In 1787 the British first attempted to establish Sierra Leone as a settlement for West Indian and American ex-slaves who had sought refuge in England (Olaudah Equiano was involved in the initial expedition there). Some of these early colonists, their numbers augmented by new black emigrants from Nova Scotia and some Maroons deported from Jamaica by the British, later moved to a new site which was named Freetown and remains the country's capital. In the 1820s Liberia was founded as a colony of freed slaves from the southern United States, who were joined by some Barbadians, and on 27 July 1847 the colony issued a Declaration of Independence. Adopting the motto "The love of liberty brought us here", Liberia became the first independent republic in Africa.

A number of Blacks from South America also settled in West Africa before the nineteenth century, and a significant number of freed slaves (*emancipados*) from Brazil and Cuba began to arrive during the early decades of the nineteenth century, many of them returning to Yorubaland in Nigeria whence their ancestors had come. Brazilians of note who came were people like Francisco Felix de Souza, Jose Domingos, Martine and Joaquin D'Almeida, who established commercial houses in West Africa. For those repatriated – like the black Brazilians – the process of assimilation was relatively complete, although various Portuguese names such as Ribeiro and Olympio persist along the coast.

The feeling of wanting to return to Africa was very strong among Blacks of the diaspora in the early decades of the twentieth century. In 1913-14 Chief Alfred Sam, a merchant from the western Gold Coast who had travelled to North America in 1911, raised $100,000 to buy a steamship to try to bring Black people from the mid-western region of the United States to West Africa. Sam's movement was not successful, but by 1916 Marcus Garvey (1887-1940) had arrived in the United States from Jamaica to found an influential movement encouraging Blacks to go back to Africa.

Garvey's Universal Negro Improvement Association was an organization with over 1,100 branches in more than forty countries. In addition to his efforts to effect the return of African peoples to Africa, Garvey promoted the idea of recognizing the importance of the Black race and of self-reliance and talked about the problems that Black people faced. He started a weekly newspaper, *The Negro World*, to propagate his views and organized a shipping company called the Black Star Line. As a result of alleged irregularities in operating the finances of the shipping line, he was deported to Jamaica in 1927. In 1939 he moved to London where he died the following year. The Garvey movement, like other back-to-Africa movements, ultimately failed, but it had significant implications for African nationalism. Many of the people of the diaspora concerned with repatriation showed an interest in African history and culture, writing books and pamphlets to show that Africa indeed had an important past and present. The philosophy of the Rastafarians of Jamaica and other parts of the Black world, whose religion developed from a belief in the divinity of the late Haile Selassie, crowned Emperor Ras Tafari I of Ethiopia in 1930, has much to do with projecting the history and culture of Africa, as well as with a literal return to the motherland.

Africans who were captured on the high seas during the abolition era and settled in Sierra Leone made a contribution to Africa as well. Dr James Africanus Beale Horton became a prominent surgeon in the West African British Medical Service. He wrote about West Africa and African nationalism, advocating self-government in 1867 in his book *West African Countries and Peoples: A Vindication of the African Race*. Another recaptive, Samuel A. Crowther, became the first African bishop of the Anglican Church in Nigeria.

A "returnee" who was perhaps the greatest intellectual figure in nineteenth-century Africa was Edward Wilmot Blyden (1832-1912). Born on the island of St Thomas in what was then the Danish West Indies, he emigrated to Liberia in 1851, later moving to Sierra Leone, and was one of the earliest advocates of Pan-Africanism, a movement which was to draw the support of many Blacks from the diaspora. The first Pan-African Conference, in London in 1900, was organized by a Trinidadian, Henry Sylvester Williams (1869-1911). Williams subsequently went to South Africa and became the first Black barrister registered in Cape Town, but finding the country uncongenial he returned to London (where he won a seat on the Marylebone Borough Council in 1906, becoming Britain's first Black local government official).

Among the Black delegates from Africa, the Caribbean and the United States attending the 1900 conference were the noted American scholar W.E.B. du Bois (1868-1953), who was to make his last home in Ghana, and George J. Christian from Dominica, who that same year went to the Gold Coast, practised as a barrister and served on the Legislative Council there until his death in 1940. In the early decades of this century the Gold Coast similarly attracted many other individuals from the West Indies who made valuable contributions in various spheres: among businessmen and professionals who came were Phipps from Trinidad, Nicholson, Shackleford, McNeill Stewart and Riley from Jamaica, Lewis and François from St Lucia, and Abbensetts, a barrister from British Guiana. Much pioneering medical work in the rural areas was done by doctors who came from the Caribbean: from Trinidad, Hoyte, Busby and Simmons; from St Lucia, Auguste and Beausoleil; from British Guiana, Murrell. Prominent in the political arena was George Padmore (1902?-59), born Malcolm Nurse in Trinidad, who became personal advisor to Ghana's first president Kwame Nkrumah, having worked for over twenty-five years for the liberation of African people. An associate of his was Guyanese-born George Nathaniel Griffith, better known by his adopted Ethiopian name of Thomas Ras Makonnen (c. 1900-84), one of the small group of West Indian and African intellectuals — including Jomo Kenyatta and Trinidadian historian C.L.R. James — who articulately advocated Pan-Africanism from the 1930s onwards. Prompted by the Italian invasion of Ethiopia, he and others of African descent formed an association in London in 1935 called the International African Friends of Abyssinia, and he became treasurer of the International African Service Bureau, founded in 1937, which was chaired by Padmore and issued a journal edited by James. In 1956 Makonnen went to live and work for ten years in Nkrumah's Ghana, later becoming a citizen of Kenya, where he died. The coming of Independence to ex-colonial countries of Africa similarly spurred many Afro-Americans to put down new roots in the continent.

Whether people of African origin stayed abroad or returned to Africa, many of them maintained a strong spiritual bond with the African continent.

The European image of Africa evolved during the era of the slave trade. Works by travellers and slave traders during this period had much to say about the cultural conditions of the "dark continent" and, although their tone ranged from sympathetic to hostile, the overall picture was unfavourable and generally showed ethnocentric contempt for the African. In spite of information to the contrary provided by abolitionist literature during the eighteenth and nineteenth centuries, the view that stressed African barbarity and depravity remained and was reinforced by the pseudo-scientific racism of the nineteenth century, which in turn influenced the organization of colonial regimes after the conquest of Africa in the late nineteenth century.

Ironically, the slave trade and its final termination in Africa contributed to this conquest. Great Britain, which had taken the lead in the suppression of the Atlantic slave trade, pursued a more active policy in Africa as her efforts to eradicate the trade led to even more involvements. British treaties with African rulers and the activities of her merchants strengthened the link with Africa. When Britain annexed Lagos, Nigeria, in 1861, part of the reason for doing so was to stamp out the slave trade. Many of the early trading posts which European nations had established on the African coast became bases for conquest during the nineteenth century, completing a savage cycle of exploitation.

7
The Impact on the Atlantic World

For over three hundred years the slave trade brought the continents of Europe, Africa and the Americas together in a commercial relationship. Although this contact was based primarily on economic factors, the millions of Africans who were brought into the Americas significantly affected the demography and culture of the New World. The subjugation and exploitation of African people as slaves resulted in their being relegated to an inferior status and made them victims of a prejudice that was justified by arguments of white supremacy. The proliferation of racism and the subsequent relegation of Blacks to a low social position, coupled with their striving to better themselves and to gain equality, have had serious socio-political implications in the United States and in Latin America.

Although it is difficult to talk of mercantilism as a consistent, enduring economic policy over three centuries of European history, in an age that lacked a corpus of systematic economics, the term conjures up certain assumptions and beliefs.[1] European governments were influenced by a concern for the balance of trade and these governments encouraged exports and discouraged the importation of manufactured goods. Mercantilist economic policy also had the object of developing an industrial, commercial and maritime superstructure from an agrarian base, for the purpose of obtaining a larger share of the profits of international commerce for its own citizens. In mercantilism, the goal of economy and polity were nearly identical. When the economy benefited, the power of the state increased, and that power was used further to enhance wealth. As a member of the British Board of Trade put it in 1726:

> Every act of a dependent provincial government ought, therefore, to terminate to the advantage of the mother state unto whom it owes its being and protection in all valuable privileges. Hence, it follows that all advantageous projects or commercial gains in any colony, which are

truly prejudical to and inconsistent with the interest of the mother state, must be understood to be illegal and the practice of them unwarrantable, because they contradict the end for which the colony had a being and are incompatible with the terms on which the people claim both privileges and protection. . . .For such is the end of the colonies, and if this use cannot be made of them it will be much better for the state to do without them.[2]

The profits from the slave trade have been linked with the industrial revolution of Britain and Eric Williams has asserted that they provided one of the main streams from the accumulation of capital in England that financed the industrial revolution. Scholars like Roger Anstey and Stanley Engerman have estimated that the contribution of slave-trade profits to capital formation in England ranged from 2.4 per cent to 10.8 per cent between 1686 and 1770.

During the eighteenth century, many of the founders of banks and insurance companies were originally associated with the triangular trade.[3] It was not uncommon during the heyday of the slave trade for a tradesman to become first a merchant and then a banker. The Heywoods, who in 1773 founded the Heywood Bank of Liverpool which they maintained until its purchase in 1883 by the Bank of Liverpool, had been successful merchants in the African trade. David and Alexander Barclay, who had participated in the American and the West Indian trade, joined with the banking families of their spouses to establish Barclay's Bank. Lloyd's of London, now the most famous insurance company in the world, insured slaves and slave ships. Industry also profited from the trade: James Watt and his steam engine were largely financed by capital accumulated from the West Indian trade.

The British mercantilist Postlethwayt described black slaves as "the fundamental prop and support" of the British colonies. In his view, the commerce of the British colonies was "a trade of . . . essential and allowed concernment to the wealth and naval power of Great Britain".[4] An eighteenth-century pamphleteer wrote in 1763:

If we resolve in our minds what an amazing variety of trades receive their daily support as many of them did originally their being, from the calls of the African and West Indian markets . . . we may from thence form a competent idea of the prodigious value of our sugar colonies and a just conception of their importance and prosperity to this their mother country.[5]

By the very nature of the slave trade, many British merchants became associated with it. The British historian L.B. Namier states:

> There were comparatively few merchants in Great Britain in 1761 who, in one connection or other, did not trade with the West Indies, and a considerable number of gentry families had interests in the Sugar Islands.[6]

Estimates of the rate of return on the slave trade and its profitability vary. Eric Williams stated that "profits of 100 per cent were not uncommon in Liverpool, and one voyage netted a clear profit of at least 300 per cent",[7] admitting, however, that overall profits averaged about 30 per cent. While other studies differ with him on the level of profitability, even the more cautious estimates indicate a lucrative business. British historian Roger Anstey, who has studied the British slave trade between 1761 and 1808, calculated that between 1791 and 1800 profits averaged 13.3 per cent and were 3.3 per cent in 1801 and 1802; this was no small return in an era of stable prices.[8] A recent study of the Liverpool slave trade by British historian David Richardson estimates the profits to have been 10 per cent, although there were fluctuations for individual voyages.[9] The Canadian historian Robert Stein also suggests that a 10 per cent return, which included French government subsidies, is a reasonable estimate for the French slave trade from Nantes in the middle of the eighteenth century.[10]

During the nineteenth century, reduced supply offered opportunities for higher profit, albeit higher risk. According to one slave trader, "the profitable result is pretty well calculated by the merchant . . . he fits out four vessels, and expects to lose three; if he should lose only two, he would consider himself lucky".[11] Actual profits of the suppressed trade during the nineteenth century ranged from 12.7 per cent to 29.6 per cent. Thus, the efficiency made necessary by the British navy patrol apparently increased the nineteenth-century trade profit by up to 100 per cent when the profits of the non-suppressed trade are estimated at 13 per cent.[12]

The slave trade involved many stages, each of which usually yielded a profit. Vessels left Europe with goods that were to be bartered for slaves in Africa. The slaves were then traded in the West Indies for sugar and, finally, the ships returned home. After 1750, specially built ships from England carried much of the sugar produced in the British West Indies, and a system of credit guarantees made it difficult to secure a return cargo for slave ships. Yet in spite of this many merchants were able to operate in the triangular trade until abolition in 1807.[13]

The slave trade brought some 9,778,000 Africans to the Americas. Brazil received 38 per cent of the total, the British Caribbean and French Caribbean 17 per cent each, Spanish America 17 per cent, the United States 6 per cent and the Dutch, Danish and Swedish Caribbean 6 per cent. This geographic distribution of slaves has little correlation with the subsequent distribution of black populations in the Americas. When the legal trade ended, the United States and Brazil had some 70 per cent of the black population in the New World. In the United States, where slave mortality was not as high as in other areas, the slave population grew from 700,000 to 4,000,000 between 1790 and 1860, while the free black population expanded from about 60,000 to 500,000.

Several factors account for the high mortality among the slave populations in Brazil and elsewhere. The low ratio of females to males precluded many unions. Even where women were available, the female fertility rate was low. Taxing physical labour during pregnancy undoubtedly increased risks of miscarriage. Low birth rates, however, were only one problem. During the period of "seasoning" in the American tropics, about 7 per cent of the slaves died in Cuba and 10 per cent in the British Caribbean. Although "creole" or native-born slaves survived better in the Americas, their numbers had to be supplemented through imports. In some areas in the Americas, Cuba and other Latin American countries the existence of unstable populations was the result of in and out migrations which caused atypical age and sex distribution, all of which made reproduction difficult. The mortality rate of slaves was attributable to harsh physical labour, combined with poor food, housing and medical care. Differential material well-being or the treatment of slaves affected their mortality. Certain areas, such as Spanish America, may well have deserved the reputation for a benign system of slavery prior to the development of the plantation system, but there is a positive correlation between slave mortality and sugar cultivation.

Some areas of Latin America witnessed a remarkable decline in black population well before emancipation, and in some sections Blacks have almost disappeared as a population group, as well as in local histories. During the first decade of the nineteenth century, the black population of Latin America comprised about 3.5 per cent of the total population, while it averaged about 60 per cent in Cuba and Puerto Rico at the time of abolition. By 1866, Blacks formed about 7 per cent of the population in the United States. They comprised 33 per cent of Brazilian inhabitants in 1890. By 1954, only 2.3 per cent of Uruguay was black. There were also similar declines in Chile, Paraguay, Peru and Mexico.[14] Today, it is rare to see people of African descent in some of these areas. The virtual disappearance of Blacks in countries such as Argentina has been attributed to the loss of males through their being drafted into revolutionary armies to battle the Spanish. The black population was unable to recoup its losses from the heavy mortality on the battlefields.

The shortage of black males often led to miscegenation, as black women secured white sexual partners. The abolition of the slave trade ended the influx of new arrivals to make up for the inability of the black population to reproduce. Another factor was an increased white immigration into Latin America, and the lessened significance of Blacks in the labour force there. Commenting on the disappearance of Blacks in the society and history of Latin America, Magnus Mörner wrote, "As far as Spanish America is concerned, historians seem to lose all interest in the Negro as soon as abolition is accomplished. In any case, he disappears almost completely from historical literature."[15]

African culture in the New World

There were significant demographic differences in the impact of Africans on the Americas, but those who came brought with them their traditions and institutions and left a cultural impact on the societies in which they settled. A description and analysis of how African cultures and societies emerged in the New World is difficult; rarely do people transfer the social systems intact from one locale to another. The development of African societies in the New World was not simply a matter of an encounter between two cultures. The slaves themselves came from diverse cultural groups that were often unequal in power. Efforts at making definite correlations between particular regions of African and black societies in the New World are problematic because it is difficult to establish an unambiguous historical connection. Nevertheless, it can be affirmed that the enslaved Africans brought knowledge and information unique to their own culture and that they developed institutions that met their needs.

Some Blacks lived on large plantations, others on small farms, still others in urban areas. Wherever they worked, the population density of Blacks, the pattern of new arrivals from Africa, the parameters set by their masters, and the Africans' assimilation of the new culture all shaped their cultural impact on the Americas. While it is frequently difficult to prove direct transfers of African culture to the New World, there were some areas in which the cultures of traditional African societies were retained with only slight variation, and a few transplanted cultures bear striking resemblance to their African counterparts.

African cultural transfers were most complete in societies founded by the runaway slaves known as "Maroons" (a name believed to derive from the Spanish word *cimarron*, which referred to domestic animals, such as cattle and pigs, that had escaped and reverted to a wild state). Although found among the creole population, Maroon settlements were most prevalent among recent black immigrants from Africa. Maroons tended to form bands that were often grouped along ethnic lines; however, when various groups came together they did not shed their ethnic identities but worked out a pattern of peaceful coexistence. A Maroon society still survives in Jamaica's mountains and the names of their legendary leaders — Cudjoe, Accompong, Quacu, Kishee, Quao — who resisted recapture after the British conquered the island in 1655, are obvious versions of names common among the Akan people of Ghana.

One of the earliest Maroon societies in the New World was that of the Bush Negroes of Dutch and French Guiana. In 1663, in order to avoid paying taxes on their slaves, the Portuguese Jews in Surinam sent them to the forest when the tax collectors came. The slaves, however, did not return. Other societies were founded in the Surinam forest in 1712, when white masters fled the arrival of French naval forces.[16] The group was divided into three tribes: the

Sarmaca, the Djukas and the Boni. The tribes were divided into clans, which were divided further into matrilineal families. The tribe consisted of several villages, each village had a council of elders and an assembly open to all adults. Each clan had its own farm land, fishing areas and hunting territory. A chief, who was civil leader and high priest, headed each tribe and was helped in both secular and judicial matters by an official known as *gran fiskari*. As with matrilineal societies in Africa, a child belonged to the mother's clan. Marriage involved consent of the bride and payment of the bride-price.

In most areas of the Americas, African societies were more fragmentary than the one just described, but the variety and diversity of backgrounds was bridged by the colour they had in common. The unity that colour gave to black culture was inevitable; even mulatto and light-skinned Blacks, who often formed the notion of a separate identity, did so only with reference to their relationship to the black community. The emerging black cultural societies retained basic elements of African culture in various forms, some of which perpetuated an African heritage. Physical characteristics, such as carvings and musical instruments, and cultural patterns, such as speech, music, folk tales and religious beliefs, are clearly linked. Many of these manifestations had to be modified or re-cast in the new socio-cultural context of the Americas.

Despite diverse ethnic backgrounds, slaves employed these elements as they came together in communities similar to those they had known in Africa. In some areas, particularly the more urban regions, slaves and free Blacks formed themselves into "nations", complete with "kings". In Brazil, the "nations" included Mandingo, Ardra and Congo. In Peru, there were fraternity houses with "kings" and "queens". Similar houses existed in Cuba. In other areas, "nations" established religious fraternities, cult groups and mutual-aid societies, sometimes adopting European elements. After emancipation, one culture or "nation" invariably triumphed over the others. In Bahia, Brazil, although other groups existed, the Nago, or Yoruba, culture predominated. Yoruba culture also held sway in Cuba. In the Gullah Islands and Virginia, traditions from the Gold Coast predominated.

Perhaps the most striking example of a blending of African tradition with influences in the Americas occurred in the area of religion. Elements of African religion that slaves brought with them often persisted underground; but whether practised openly or surreptitiously this religion was a powerful force in their lives. These beliefs continued in both linear traditions and in syncretic combinations. Gods that had been tied to individual families in Africa became group cults in the Americas. The *orishas* (gods) of the Yoruba (Western Nigeria) survived in Cuba in the Santeriá religion and in Candomblé and Shango worship in Bahia, Brazil. In Trinidad Shango and the related religion of the Shouting Baptists, still remain a strong influence. Vodun, the Fon (from Dahomey, or present-day Benin) word for god, persisted in Haiti in particular.

African religious survivals were especially pronounced in the Spanish and Portuguese areas, where the Roman Catholic Church was most powerful. Slaves subverted the major Catholic feasts into occasions for observing their own inherited rites. All Souls' Eve (Hallowe'en) became a time for ancestor worship, and Easter week became a period of mourning for dead ancestors. In Jamaica, the Christmas-time festival of John Cunnu (variously spelled John Canoe or Jonkonnu) was thought to have been inspired by tales of a celebrated African hero who flourished in the early eighteenth-century Gold Coast. The slaves also established correlations between African gods and various Christian saints, which in some cases were personifications of natural elements. Examples include the Haitian Saint Soleil (St Sun) and Saint Lune (St Moon). Some saints who assumed anthropomorphic features, such as Saint Bouleverse (the saint of destruction), were believed to have the power to rearrange and destroy the world. Like many African gods, Saint Bouleverse, it was believed, had the capacity for both good and evil. A Haitian ode explains:

> Saint Bouleverse, you who have the power to overturn the earth, you are a saint and me, I am a sinner. I invoke you to be my patron saint from this day forward. I send you to look for someone; upset his head, upset his memory, confuse his thought, upset his house, confuse his visible and invisible. Make lightning and thunder fall upon my enemies.[17]

In many cases, Christian religious figures were even more directly equated with African gods. In Cuba, the Yoruba sky god Obatala became Jesus Christ; Sàngo, the Yoruba god of thunder, was identified with St John, while Yansan, the storm goddess, was equated with St Barbara in Brazil. Thus, when Blacks worshipped in Catholic churches displaying lithographs and statuettes of saints they were, in fact, often worshipping African divinities. In predominantly Protestant areas, where more thorough catechism training and indoctrination were provided before baptism and confirmation, African gods failed to survive as openly as in the Catholic communities.

Black magic also survived the passage from Africa, coexisting with Christianity. *Obeah*, which in the New World signified magic, came no doubt from the West African Akan word *obayifo* (witch). Obeah men and women were alleged to have the power to kill, cure or secure someone's love. Like their African counterparts, the New World obeah were believed to be able to fly, to turn themselves into animals and to suck the blood of their victims.

Nevertheless, Africans in the Americas interpreted Protestantism and the Bible according to their own sentiments, needs and understanding and created a unique form of Christianity. They compared their plight with Israel's bondage in Egypt and saw in Moses a deliverer. They identified with Israel's Babylonian captivity and longed for prophets of salvation to lead them back to freedom. They also identified with the poor and disinherited who were to be saved by the Gospel and the coming of the Lord. Their own oppression as slaves gave them a depth of religious feeling that informed and affected their songs. Spirituals such as the following became the unique cry of those in bondage (and often also had a hidden meaning, as in the first example, which served as an announcement of a meeting at the river):

> Deep river,
> My home is over Jordan,
> Deep river,
> Lord, I want to pass over into camp ground.
> Lord, I want to pass into camp ground.
> Lord, I want to pass into camp ground,
> Deep river,
> Lord, I want to pass over into camp ground.

• • •

O, don't you want to go to that gospel feast,
That promised land where all is peace.

O, when I get to Heaven I'll walk all about,
There's nobody there for to turn me out.

• • •

When Israel was in Egypt's land,
Let my people go!
Oppressed so hard they could not stand,
Let my people go!
Go down, Moses,
Tell old Pharaoh
Let my people go!

• • •

Soon will I be done with the troubles of the world,
Troubles of the world!
Soon will I be done with the troubles of the world,
Going home to live with God.

• • •

Swing low, sweet chariot,
Coming for to carry me home,
Swing low, sweet chariot,
Coming for to carry me home.
I looked over Jordan and what did I see
Coming for to carry me home?
A band of angels coming after me,
Coming for to carry me home.

The Afro-American music historian Hildred Roach has stated:
"One of the most direct influences of Africa was found in the
diverse and difficult rhythms of spirituals. Based upon the rhythms
of drum and dance as well as emotional spontaneity, they spun into

movements which encouraged foot reactions similar to the contagion of jazz as well as vocal communion among the slave population. Inherent within the spirituals were such dance rhythms as the shout, the bamboula and both religious and secular influences."[18] In terms of form, melodic variety and expressiveness, the spiritual was perhaps the most highly developed form of black folk song in America.

Music and dancing, important in Africa, indeed emerged strongly in Black America too. Whereas European music is based primarily on a single rhythm at a time, that of the African was usually characterized by a rhythmic complexity which simultaneously involved as many as four distinctly different time signatures. This use of polymeter, in addition to the employment of antiphony in singing, rasping and the playing of musical instruments in both religious and secular activities, reappeared within a new cultural context in the Americas. In Africa a master drummer often lined out rhythm in concert with his assistants, who intervened with the cross-beats; and although use of the African drum continued in the New World, it was sometimes replaced by intensive use of clapping, rattles and sticks. Musical instruments of African origin, such as the banjo, calabash, drums, types of xylophone and thumb-pianos, as well as special dance formations, all survived the passage to the Americas. The survival of the drum, which in slave societies, as in Africa, not only had a role in religion and entertainment but was used to communicate messages, and was therefore banned by slave masters throughout the Americas who felt threatened by the African ability to "talk" through it, testifies to its crucial importance.

A legacy of the African vocal tradition in secular music were work songs, which could be heard from groups of Blacks on plantations engaged, for example, in field work or harvesting. One worker might take the lead and improvise a verse, with the others joining in a chorus, in the typical call-and-response style, punctuated by rhythmic body movements such as the swinging of axes or pulling on a rope, according to the particular activity being undertaken. The following example would have been sung to accompany corn-husking:

> Five can't ketch me and ten can't hold me, Ho. . .
> Round the corn, Sally!
> *Refrain*:
> Round the corn, round the corn,
> round the corn, Sally,
> Ho, ho, ho, round the corn, Sally!

Paul Oliver has commented: "Such work songs are to be found in all parts of Africa where co-ordinated labour is required or where the rhythm of the work itself gives the basis of song."[19]

According to John Miller Chernoff, "The tradition of using songs to express philosophical, ethical, or satirical themes is so much a part of African musical idioms that it has continued, along with many rhythmic characteristics, within the development of Afro-American styles, and songs continue to serve as guides in practical philosophy to the people who listen to them."[20] The evidence for this is to be found in various types of social songs —

> Some folk say a preacher won't steal,
> I caught two in my corn field —

and parallels can be drawn with the Trinidadian calypso or kaiso (incidentally, a word believed to be an adaptation of *kaito*, a Hausa encouragement similar to "bravo").

Probably the most widespread of the songs bred by the Black experience, however, are the blues, which came to the fore in the late nineteenth century, developing from earlier forms, and have evolved as a continuing influence on all Afro-American music. Making use of "blue notes" (flattened sevenths) and a distinctive tonality that can be said to have "derived from African scales and vocal approximations and tones",[21] "the blues" express sadness and sorrowful sentiments often interspersed with a dry humour:

> Sometimes I feel like nothin', somethin' th'owed away,
> Sometimes I feel like nothin', somethin' th'owed away,
> Then I get my guitar and blow the blues all day.

> •   •   •

> I'm going down and lay my head on the railroad track,
> I'm going down and lay my head on the railway track,
> When the train come along, I'm gonna snatch it back.

• • •

Yaller gal make a preacher lay his Bible down,
Yaller gal make a preacher lay his Bible down,
Good lookin' high brown make him run from town to town. . . .

Beyond the music was the African tradition of folklore and oratory. Fulfilling the functions both of entertainment and instruction, African folktales often featured animal "trickster" figures that are the direct antecedents of characters such as Brer Rabbit in the American *Uncle Remus* stories, and of the Anancy stories of Jamaica and other parts of the Caribbean, Ananse being the wily spider in the original Asante stories. The didactic nature of folklore, the manner of its presentation and also the use of formal speech patterns left an impact. In the United States the call-and-response pattern, the yea-saying and the repetition of utterances made by leaders are found in Black speech in and out of the church, as well as in the delivery of Afro-American "soul" singers. This call-and-response style, a major characteristic of much African music and oratory, is retained in the exhortations and chanting that respond to the Black preacher: "Yeah, yeah," "I hear you," "Go ahead," "Take your time and tell it," "Look out now," "Come out with it," "Watch yourself," "Say so," "You on the case," "Uh-huh, uh-huh," and so on.

Following the folklore tradition, some of the best sermons are in the form of biblical storytelling:

Jesus told a story about labourers hired to work in a vineyard. When I was a pastor in the cotton country there was a certain block where there were people standing around all the time — any hour. And most of them were not leisure class. Leisurely folk don't dress like they did. Some had paper-sack lunches, but they were looking for no picnic. But you could tell what they were about if you would go down to the block at four or five o'clock in the morning, just before day, a big old raggedy bus would pull through there, and a man would hire folks to chop cotton. If you would watch long enough sometimes, the bus would come again and fill up again. They would work a long day in the fields and the bus would bring them back to the block around six or seven o'clock at night. Well, this is the way it was. Jesus said the man hired a load and took them to the field. But he saw it wasn't enough, so he came back in the block three hours later and hired some more. And again, even in mid-afternoon, and finally just an hour before quitting time, he came and hired some more.[22]

The folk nature was also evident in prayers and many of these phrases are still heard in Black churches today:

Now, Lord, now, Lord, when I come to the end of my journey.
When I've walked the last mile of the way.
When this world can offer me a home no longer.
When, Lord, I'm done going out and coming in.
When I've sung my last song and prayed my last prayer.
Meet me at the River Jordan and cross me over in a calm tide.

In terms of actual vocabulary, some linguists such as J. L. Dillard have claimed African roots for Americanisms such as: jive, jam (session), to dig, guy, jazz, hip, bogus, jitterbug, boogiewoogie, ofay, honkie, OK.

The legacy of African people in the Americas was also expressed authentically in food, and they made a major contribution to Creole and Southern cooking. Conditions and necessity in America, as well as the composite of methods employed by different tribal groups, led Blacks to modify their culinary style into what was called for a long time "down home" cooking but has become known as "soul food".

Although the dishes that the slaves brought varied depending on the regions from which they came, there were certain similarities. Sauces and spices were essential to successful West African cooking. They were usually prepared with hot peppers, salt, onion, garlic, vinegar, lemon, seeds, nuts and oils; and each piece of food was invariably dipped in a sauce before being placed in the mouth. The use of seeds and nuts to flavour stews was particularly African and the palm oil found in West Africa was fundamental to food preparation. Vegetables were also important and were often added to soups, stews and sauces. The impact of African culinary art in the Americas cannot be denied. While simplicity and economy were major considerations in the era of slavery, "soul food" has grown into a legitimate, not to say delicious, cuisine that employs primarily country-flavoured vegetables, eaten with corn bread, biscuits and deep-fried foods, and relies on pork in all forms as its main meat.[23]

The distinct style of Afro-American cooking initially became the diet of the poverty-stricken inhabitants of the Southern United States. Typical soul food included chitterlings, mustard greens, racks of pig's ear, black-eyed peas, hot sweet potato, fried pies and pot liquor. The daily fare of corn and pork leaving was varied occasionally with fresh-caught fish. A large number of women made do for their families with natural foods like collards, kale, turnip tips, roots, beans and sometimes racoons and possums.

Peanuts, or groundnuts, were also heavily featured in Black cooking. Although not indigenous to Africa, once introduced there the people made use of them, particularly in preparing chicken dishes. When Southerners began to grow peanuts as fodder for pigs, slaves used some of them to supplement their meals in the cabin. Many of the slaves' innovative ways with the peanut were adapted for the master's table: peanut-butter and jelly sandwiches, in butter bread, biscuits and muffins, and peanut candies and cakes.

In the Caribbean, too, many ingredients and dishes were introduced from West Africa, sometimes retaining names which are close approximations of the original African words: ackee, akkra, dokonu, okra, yam.

The Black family
Even as Black culture survived, adapted or was recreated in the New World, social organizations such as the family survived despite the assault inflicted under the exigencies of slavery. Families were often separated through sales. The Black woman was abused sexually by the men on the plantation:

> She was to be had for the taking. Boys on and about the plantation inevitably learned to use her, and having acquired the habit, often continued it into manhood and after marriage. For she was natural and could give herself up to passion in a way impossible to wives inhibited by puritanical training.[24]

The family, notwithstanding the deleterious effect of slavery whereby masters could separate couples and the authority of the master nullified parental authority, remained an important part of slave community life. Recent discussion of evidence from narratives and correspondence of slaves suggests that the family was crucial as a sustaining force for survival in slavery.[25] As the historian John Blassingame put it:

> The family, while it had no legal existence in slavery, was in actuality one of the most important survival mechanisms for the slave. In his family he found companionship, love, sexual gratification, sympathetic understanding of his sufferings. . . .The important thing was not that the family was not recognized legally or that masters frequently encouraged monogamous mating arrangements in the quarters only when it was convenient to do so, but rather that some form of family life did exist among slaves.[26]

At times, slave owners encouraged strong family discipline and stability, feeling that such cohesion among the slaves lessened the chance of individuals running away from the plantations. Thus, far from being crushed by the experience of slavery, Blacks created societies and institutions that helped them cope with their conditions in the Americas.

Prejudice and white supremacy

European expansion and dominance, and the subjugation of black people, resulted in attitudes, ideologies and policies that strengthened the notion of Caucasian superiority. However, the idea of black inferiority was present even before the establishment of large slave societies in the Americas. For example, racial prejudice existed in the Arab world where trading activities in the trans-Saharan area and in East Africa preceded the Atlantic slave trade and slavery in the New World. In the Arab world, the word '*abd* originally meant "slave", without colour distinction, but it later came to mean black slave, until finally the word was applied to black people in general — enslaved or free.[27]

In Portugal, the first European country directly to import African slaves by sea, racial prejudice was manifested early. In 1515, Blacks in Portugal were experiencing serious difficulties in getting their dead buried; in response the king ordered that black corpses be thrown into a separate con.mon ditch.[28] This early prejudice was further reinforced in Europe in the late nineteenth century by the pseudo-scholarly opinion of historians, philosophers, scientists and psychologists, so it is hardly surprising that slave societies established by European countries in the New World perpetuated the view of black inferiority. In fact, racial prejudice was no less pronounced in one area than another. Too much has probably been made of Portuguese racial policy and intermarriage, sometimes leading scholars to interpret this as lack of prejudice in Portuguese colonies. As C. R. Boxer suggests: "it did not follow from this readiness to mate with coloured women, that the Portuguese male had not racial prejudice".[29] Race mixture in Portuguese colonies arose because it was expedient. Whether under slavery or after slavery, white males have sexually exploited and abused black women, while at the same time trying to protect their own women from sexual contact with black men.

While prejudice was universal in all slave societies, the New World saw variations in patterns of racial classification. In the United States, the races were divided between white and black, and there was no assumption of intermediate status connected with intermediate colour. But an intermediate or mulatto group did emerge in the European slave colonies, and in these New World societies the lightest of the mulattos were acknowledged socially. This three-tier racial classification can be explained as a result of economics, class and prejudice. The division within the Black world mirrored the racism encountered by a black society living among whites. Mulattos, though not viewed as a separate race in the United States, often regarded themselves as such. In North America, mulatto slaves were often given privileged positions as house servants and artisans, and their position in these areas of employment was disproportionate to their numbers. The field slaves were predominately black.

Racial prejudice increased in the post-abolition period, and racial inequality was a result of social inequality. In Brazil, particularly in southern Brazil, many freed slaves became sharecroppers, turning to a subsistence agriculture that gave them a marginal existence. Their status as free men, however, neither enhanced their social position nor removed the stigma of inferiority.[30] Florestan Fernandes, the Brazilian sociologist, wrote concerning Brazil:

> If we take the network of race relations in our times as a frame of reference, it might appear that the economic, social, and political inequality existing between the Negro and the white were the fruit of

colour prejudice and racial discrimination. However, historical-sociological analysis makes it clear that these mechanisms have another function: that of maintaining social distance between races and the corresponding pattern of sociocultural isolation of the Negro, which are preserved together as a whole by the mere unrestricted perpetuation of archaic segmental structure.[31]

Psuedo-scientific evidence lent support to the idea that Blacks were morally and intellectually inferior to Whites, and many Whites have yet to liberate their minds from the racism and prejudice that the slave trade and its consequences fostered, which has led not only to their segregation of Blacks on the basis of race but also to their subjugation and suppression. To a large degree, colour determined the social conditions of Blacks in the New World and the very limits and range of opportunities open to them.

While the problem of prejudice remained after emancipation, it has been swept under the rug in Latin America. Because legal segregation, such as existed in the United States, is not applied there, certain Blacks in Latin America claim not to feel the effects of discrimination. Nevertheless, in Spanish America, the Blacks and mulattos are not counted among the "in" and are among the "have nots" everywhere.

In contrast to the situation in Latin America since emancipation, Blacks in the United States have fought to change the disabilities imposed on them through segregation laws dating from the 1890s. The thrust to change conditions came primarily from those who had managed to educate themselves: black professionals, doctors, lawyers and teachers; and out of these groups came a new leadership which demanded equal rights and opportunities of citizenship for all.

The disenfranchisement and segregation of Blacks in the South, where most of them lived in the 1890s, was reinforced by national apathy and the need of Southern Democrats to insulate themselves from class-based third-party challenges. The recognized spokesperson of the period was Booker T. Washington, black president of The Tuskegee Institute in Alabama. Born into slavery in 1856 Washington proposed that Blacks improve their position through education without demanding a change in status and that they make the best of the position to which they had been relegated.

Blacks were to learn trades, be good tenant farmers and fit into their "places". Thus, Blacks would become an entity before demanding recognition. He told them, "Cast down your bucket where you are." This was the so-called Atlanta Compromise of 1895.

Washington's programme was attacked by William E.B. Du Bois, a young sociologist, born in Massachusetts of free black ancestors. He earned a Ph.D. from Harvard, studied in Germany and taught at Atlanta University. He objected to the Atlanta Compromise as creating "Uncle Toms" and what he called "white man's niggers". Du Bois took part in the Niagara Movement, organized at Niagara Falls in 1905, to obtain citizenship rights and liberal, rather than only trade school, education for Blacks.

More important in the quest for equality was the development of the National Association for the Advancement of Colored People (NAACP), founded as a result of the 1908 race riots in Springfield, Illinois, which resulted in the death of scores of Blacks and drove others out of town. The NAACP, formed in 1909, was an organization whose leadership was initially largely white. In 1910, the Urban League, an organization devoted to Blacks in urban areas was formed.

In spite of serious efforts, however, changes were minimal before the 1960s, when there emerged a new black leadership. This leadership came from a source of strength that the Afro-American had looked to through the long years of oppression — religion and the church. Few could object to hymn-singing at a bus-stop or make a crime of praying on courthouse steps in the so-called Bible belt of the United States where most Blacks lived. Thus, from the pulpits and pews of Black churches came a new leadership endowed with faith and a willingness to suffer the consequences of protesting unjust laws. Among the many people who contributed to the movement to gain civil rights, an outstanding leader in the 1960s was the Reverend Martin Luther King, Jr. (1929-68). It was the pacificism of King, who studied the philosophies of Christ and Gandhi and put them into practice in the South, that altered the status quo. Blacks were shot, bombed, insulted and tear-gassed, but they used the courts and the jails in the best revolutionary American tradition to get laws changed, schools opened and seats in the *front* of the bus.

One of those who helped awaken Afro-Americans to a new consciousness was Malcolm X. Born in 1925, the son of a staunch Garveyite, Malcolm renounced his "slave name" of Little when he became a Black Muslim, after learning about Islam during a prison sentence. In 1964, having left the movement, he organized the first Muslim Mosque, Inc., and later founded the non-religious Organization of Afro-American Unity. Not long after returning from a trip abroad, he was assassinated in New York on 21 February 1965 — as Martin Luther King was to be three years later.

The quest of Afro-Americans to change their condition in the United States went a stage further when, in 1966, they began to define their aspirations in terms of "Black Power", a phrase used significantly that year by Stokely Carmichael (who after his marriage in 1968 to South African singer Miriam Makeba went to live in Conakry, Guinea, and later became known as Kwame Turé) then chairman of the Student Nonviolent Coordinating Committee (SNCC). This movement sought to define the meaning of Black consciousness within the limits imposed on African peoples in American society in the context of racism, prejudice and politics. It was, in part, a recognition of the fact that Blacks had to find their identity not in the slave experience but in relationship to their African heritage. The idea of Black Power itself was not a totally new concept. Black people in the United States had never lost completely their spiritual relationship with Africa. They had maintained some contacts through the settlement of Liberia, through the interest of individual Black Americans in Africa during the nineteenth century, through the Pan-Africanism movement and the movement of the Jamaican-born Marcus Garvey, who sought to lead Blacks back to Africa. This spiritual relationship between Africa and her children is probably most famously embodied in the personal quest of the writer Alex Haley, who was able to trace and document his African ancestry back to its roots in the village of Juffure, in the Gambia.[32] In the United States, black became *Black*, as racial pride was slowly restored and opportunities were painfully acquired.

Black people in the Americas, in spite of their long presence there, have not on the whole become fully part of the societies into which they were imported. In the Caribbean, where much poverty persists with little chance of amelioration, many have embarked on a search for better opportunities in North America and Europe. Whether Blacks in the Americas stayed and tried to improve their lot within the societies which originally imported them or whether they searched for a brighter future in other areas, they did so for the most part with courage, dignity and hope. These human beings who were brutally torn from their people and exchanged in a savage trade that brought them in their millions to the New World in dark, crowded, stifling dungeons, who were sold as slaves to hostile masters for whatever their flesh would bring, were nevertheless able to stand the storm of their life and times as a people.

Notes and Sources

(For fuller publication details, consult Select Bibliography.)

Introduction (pp. 1-4)

A good place to start on the large number of resources available for the study of the slave trade are two useful bibliographies: P.C. Hogg, *The African Slave Trade and Suppression: A Classified and Annotated Bibliography* (1973), which covers much of the literature on the subject up to 1967, and J.C. Miller, *Slavery: A Comparative Teaching Bibliography* (1977). Miller's book concentrates on the period since 1900 and contains a comprehensive listing of literature on the slave trade published in the 1960s and 1970s. A supplement to this useful guide is provided in J.C. Miller and D.H. Borus, "Slavery: A Supplementary Teaching Bibliography", in *Slavery and Abolition*, I, 1 (1980), pp.65-110. C. Fyfe's "A Historiographical Survey", in *The Transatlantic Slave Trade from West Africa* (1965), also contains a good discussion of historical writings on the subject.

A number of works provide access to the documents and the primary and secondary sources dealing with the slave trade. E. Donnan (ed.), *Documents Illustrative of the History of the Slave Trade to America* (4 vols, 1930-35), gives the most detailed compendium presently available of source material. Other worthwhile, shorter collections include M. Craton, J. Walvin and D. Wright, *Slavery, Abolition and Emancipation* (1976); G.F. Dow, *Slave Ships and Slaving* (1927); R.W. Beachy, *A Collection of Documents on the Slave Trade of Eastern Africa* (1976); and P.D. Curtin (ed.), *Africa Remembered: Narratives of West Africans from the Era of the Slave Trade* (1967).

Among the collections of essays on many facets of the trade and abolition are: C. Bolt and S. Drescher, *Anti-Slavery, Religion and Reform* (1980); H. Gemery and J. Hogendorn (eds), *The Uncommon Market: Essays on the Slave Trade* (1979); W.E. Minchinton and P.C. Emmer (eds), *The Atlantic Trade: New Approaches* (1976), M.L. Kilson and R.I. Rotberg (eds), *The African Diaspora: Interpretive Essays* (1976); R.T. Anstey and P.E.H. Hair (eds), *Liverpool: The African Slave Trade and Abolition* (1977); S.L. Engerman and E. Genovese (eds), *Race and Slavery*

(1977); V. Rubin and A. Tuden (eds), "Comparative Perspectives on Slavery in New World Plantation Societies", in *Annals of the New York Academy of Science* (1977).

Much recent research on the slave trade has been quantitative in nature, P.D. Curtin's pioneer study *The Atlantic Slave Trade: A Census* (1969) has stimulated some substantive research, including works by J. Postma, "The Dimension of the Dutch Slave Trade from Western Africa", in *Journal of African History* (1972), "The Dutch Slave Trade: A Quantitative Assessment", in Minchinton and Emmer's *Atlantic Slave Trade*, and "The Origin of African Slaves: The Dutch Activities on the Guinea Coast, 1675-1795", in Engerman and Genovese's *Race and Slavery;* J.C. Miller, "Legal Portuguese Slaving from Angola: Some Preliminary Indications of Volume and Direction, 1760-1830", in Minchinton and Emmer's *Atlantic Slave Trade*; P. Manning, "The Slave Trade in Southern Dahomey", and D. Eltis, "The Direction and Fluctuation of the Trans-Atlantic Slave Trade, 1821-1843; A Revision of the 1845 Parliamentary Paper", both in Gemery and Hogendorn's *Uncommon Market*. H.S. Klein, *The Middle Passage* (1978), provides a competent study from a quantitative and a comparative perspective. Curtin's conclusions about the numbers involved in the trade have been supplemented and revised by such works as R.T. Anstey's "The Volume and Profitability of the British Slave Trade, 1761-1810", in Engerman and Genovese, *Race and Slavery*, and "The Volume of the North American Slave-Carrying Trade from Africa, 1761-1810", in Minchinton and Emmer, *Atlantic Slave Trade*. Particularly critical is J.E. Inikori, "Measuring the Atlantic Slave Trade", in *Journal of African History* (1976), a response to which appears in the same issue (pp.595-627) in P.D. Curtin, R.T. Anstey and J.E. Inikori, "Discussion: Measuring the Atlantic Slave Trade". Works which slightly modify Curtin's figures but not his conclusions include D. Eltis, "The Transatlantic Slave Trade, 1821-1843" (1978), and P. Lovejoy, *Transformations of Slavery* (1983).

Besides specialized works, there are many competent surveys of the history of the slave trade with varying purposes and scope. These include: B. Davidson, *Black Mother: The Years of the African Slave Trade* (1961); D.P. Mannix and M. Cowley, *Black Cargoes: A History of the Atlantic Slave Trade 1518–1865* (1962); J. Pope-Hennessey, *Sins of the Fathers: A Study of the Atlantic Slave Traders* (1967); O. Ransford, *The Slave Trade: The Story of Transatlantic Slavery* (1971); C. Duncan Rice, *The Rise and Fall of Black Slavery* (1971); J.A. Rawley, *The Transatlantic Slave Trade* (1981).

1. For an assessment of this movement in a global perspective see George E. Shepperson, "The African Abroad or the African Diaspora", in T.O.

Ranger (ed.). *Emerging Themes in African History* (Nairobi, 1968), pp. 152-76, his introduction to Kilson and Rotberg, *African Diaspora* (Cambridge, 1976), and J.E. Harris, *Global Dimensions of the African Diaspora* (Washington DC, 1982).

2. See R.A. Austen, "The Trans-Saharan Slave Trade: A Tentative Census", in Gemery and Hogendorn, *Uncommon Market* (New York, 1979), pp.23-76.

3. See Esmond B. Martin and T.C.I. Ryan, "A Quantitative Assessment of the Arab Slave Trade of East Africa, 1770-1896", in *Kenya Historical Review*, vol.5 (1977), pp.71-91. A more rigorous assessment is provided in R.A. Austen, "The Islamic Slave Trade out of Africa (Red Sea and Indian Ocean): An Effort at Quantification", paper presented at Conference on Islamic Africa: Slavery and Related Institutions, Princeton University, June 1977; R.W. Beachy, *The Slave Trade of Eastern Africa* (London, 1976), and M.D.W. Nwulia, *Britain and Slavery in East Africa* (Washington, DC, 1976).

1: African Slavery and African Society (pp. 5-27)

The historical literature on African slavery has been growing in recent years. A masterful study is Lovejoy's *Transformations in Slavery;* his "Indigenous African Slavery", in *Historical Reflections*, 6, 1 (1979), pp.19-83, and *Ideology of Slavery in Africa* (1981) are also well worth reading. Among the older and still useful works is J. Nieboer, *Slavery as an Industrial System* (1900). W. Rodney's "African Slavery and Other Forms of Social Oppression on the Upper Guinea Coast in the Context of the Atlantic Slave-Trade", in *Journal of African History* (1966), is an important article. J.D. Fage's "Slavery and the Slave Trade in the Context of West African History", in *Journal of African History* (1969), is a stimulating summary. Wrigley's "Historicism in Africa", in *African Affairs* (1971), is a response to Fage. An analysis of published European accounts of institutions of servitude from Senegal to Angola between about 1445 and 1700 is provided in J.D. Fage, "Slaves and Society in Western Africa", in *Journal of African Studies* (1980). Two of the most important books are C. Meillassoux (ed.), *L'esclavage en Afrique pré-coloniale* (1975), which looks at slavery in West Africa as a mode of production, and S. Miers and I. Kopytoff (eds.), *Slavery in Africa: Historical and Anthropological Perspectives* (1977), which considers slavery in terms of kinship structures. The views of Miers and Kopytoff are criticized in M. Klein, "The Study of Slavery in Africa: A Review Article", in *Journal of African History* (1978), and F. Cooper, "Studying Slavery in Africa: Some Criticisms and Comparisons", in *Journal of African History* (1979). R. Harms, "Slave Systems in Africa", in *History in Africa* (1978), is also valuable. A stimulating set of essays is J.L. Watson (ed.), *Asian and African Systems of Slavery* (1980). O. Patterson's *Slavery and Social Death* (1982) is another important work.

A good place to start on the environment in which African societies functioned is W. Fitzgerald, *Africa: A Social, Economic and Political Geography of its Major Regions* (1967), and W.A. Hance, *The Geography of Modern Africa* (1941). An excellent overview is to be found in G.P. Murdock, *Africa: Its People and their Cultural History* (1959). E.P. Skinner (ed.), *Peoples and Cultures of Africa* (1973), is also useful. Excellent studies of African political systems include D. Forde and P.M. Kaberry, *West African Kingdoms in the Nineteenth Century* (1967); M. Fortes and E.E. Evans-Pritchard, *African Political Systems* (1940); and J. Middleton and D. Tait, *Tribes Without Rulers* (1958). African religions and world views receive attention in W.E. Abraham, *The Mind of Africa* (1962); D. Forde (ed.), *African Worlds* (1954); W.T. Harris and H. Sawyer, *The Springs of Mende Belief and Conduct* (1969), and their *Concepts of God in Africa* (1970); K.A. Opoku, *West African Traditional Religion* (1978); E.G. Parrinder, *West African Religion* (1961); H. Sawyer, *God: Ancestor or Creator* (1970); and V.C. Uchendu, *The Igbo of Southeast Nigeria* (1965). Among the basic studies that conveniently survey African arts are F. Willett, *African Art* (1968), E. Lenzinger, *The Art of Black Africa* (1972), and J. Vansina, *Art History in Africa* (1984). Two indispensable books on African music are F. Bebey's *African Music: A People's Art* (1975) and J.H.K. Nketia's *The Music of Africa* (1974).

1. See R.S. Rattray, *Ashanti Law and Constitution* (London, 1929), pp.34-46; E. Reynolds, *Trade and Economic Change on the Gold Coast, 1807-1874* (London, 1974), pp.18-19.
2. See Nieboer, *Slavery as an Industrial System* (The Hague, 1900), p.5.
3. Although the present discussion describes the process of recruiting slaves in non-Muslim societies, a similar practice prevailed in Islamic societies in Africa. On recruitment, see Miers and Kopytoff, *Slavery in Africa* (Madison, 1977), pp.12-14. On African slavery in Muslim societies, see A.G.B. Fisher and H.J. Fisher, *Slavery and Muslim Society in Africa* (London, 1970).
4. See Miers and Kopytoff, *Slavery in Africa*, pp.55-9; Meillassoux, *L'esclavage en Afrique pré-coloniale;* M. Klein and P. Lovejoy, "Slavery in West Africa", in Gemery and Hogendorn, *Uncommon Market*, pp. 181-212.
5. See J. Vogt, *Portuguese Rule on the Gold Coast* (Athens, 1979), p.72.

6. Ray A. Kea, "Gold Production and Trade: Aspects of Social-Economic Development in the Gold Coast Historical Formation during the Sixteenth and Seventeenth Centuries", paper read at 19th annual meeting of African Studies Association, November 1979.

7. See Ivor Wilks, *Asante in the Nineteenth Century* (Cambridge, 1975), pp.435-6.

8. See Nehemia Levtzion, "The Western Maghrib and the Sudan", in R. Oliver, *Cambridge History of Africa*, Vol.3 (London, 1975), p.447.

9. See ibid., p.386.

10. See Klein and Lovejoy, "Slavery in West Africa", in Gemery and Hogendorn, *Uncommon Market*, pp. 192-3.

11. See V. Uchendu, "Slaves and Slavery in Igboland, Nigeria", in Miers and Kopytoff, *Slavery in Africa*, p.130.

12. T. Canot, *Captain Canot, or Twenty Years of an African Slaver* (London, 1854).

13. Rodney, "African Slavery and Other Forms of Social Oppression on the Upper Guinea Coast in the Context of the Atlantic Slave Trade", in *Journal of African History*, 7 (1966), pp.431-44. Fage, "Slaves and Society in Western Africa, c.1445-c.1700", in *Journal of African History*, 21 (1980), has examined the extent to which institutions of servitude on the coast between Senegal and Angola were autonomous developments or a response to European demand for slaves.

14. While some slave societies like those in Asia could be characterized as closed, Africa had both closed and open slave systems and it was often possible to incorporate acquired outsiders into the society. For a discussion of both systems, see Watson, *Asian and African Systems of Slavery* (Oxford, 1980), pp.9-13. On the incorporation of the outsider in Africa, see Miers and Kopytoff, *Slavery in Africa*, pp.22-49.

15. See Miers and Kopytoff, *Slavery in Africa*, p.15.

16. See V. Uchendu, "Slavery in Southeast Nigeria", and D. McCall, "Slavery in Ashanti, Ghana", both in *Transaction*, January-February 1967, pp.52-4 and 55-6.

17. See J.C. Miller, "Imbangala Lineage Slavery", and W. MacGaffey, "Economic and Social Dimensions of Kongo Slavery", both in Miers and Kopytoff, *Slavery in Africa*, pp.205-33 and 235-57.

18. See J.H. Vaughan, "Mafakur: A Limbic Institution of the Margi", in Miers and Kopytoff, *Slavery in Africa*, pp.85-102.

19. See Thomas Tlon, "Servility and Political Control: Botlhanka among the Batawana of Northern Botswana, c.1750-1906", in Miers and Kopytoff, *Slavery in Africa*, pp.367-88.

20. Cruickshank, *Eighteen Years on the Gold Coast of Africa*, vol.2 (London, 1853), p.240.

21. Ibid., p.228.
22. Ibid., p.233.
23. Ibid., p.228.
24. For further discussion, see Cooper, "Studying Slavery in Africa", in *Journal of African History*, Vol.20, no.1 (1979), pp.103-25.
25. See Jean Hiernaux, *The People of Africa* (New York, 1975).
26. See Joseph H. Greenberg, *The Languages of Africa* (Bloomington, 1963).
27. On kinship, see A.R. Radcliffe-Brown and D. Forde (eds.), *African Systems of Kinship and Marriage* (London, 1950), and Skinner, *Peoples and Cultures of Africa* (New York, 1973), section III.
28. Opoku, *West African Traditional Religion* (Accra, 1978), pp.104-22, 124-5.
29. R.S. Wassing and Hans Hinz, *African Art* (New York, 1971), p.199.
30. Curt Sachs, *A History of Musical Instruments* (New York, 1940), p.455.
31. Bebey, *African Music* (New York, 1975), p.115.
32. Ibid., p.128.
33. Ibid., p.134.
34. Nketia, *Music of Africa* (New York, 1974), p.217.
35. Roland Oliver and Brian Fagan, *Africa in the Iron Age, c.500 B.C. to A.D. 1400* (Cambridge, 1975), provides a comprehensive study on the use and spread of iron in Africa.
36. Useful accounts of the traditional economy may be found in Lars Sunstrom, *The Guinea Trade* (Oslo, 1966), Reynolds, *Trade and Economic Change*, and A.G. Hopkins, *An Economic History of West Africa* (London, 1973).
37. See Middleton and Tait, *Tribes Without Rulers*, pp.1-30.
38. See Shapera, *Government and Polities in Tribal Societies* (London, 1956), p.220.
39. See Wilks, *Asante*.
40. See Mair, *African Kingdoms* (London, 1977), pp.66-72.
41. See Fortes and Evans-Pritchard, *African Political Systems* (London, 1967), pp.xiv-xix.

2: The Slave Trade (pp. 28-46)

The best sources for studying the early Atlantic trade are G. Eannes de Azurara, *The Chronicle of the Discovery and Conquest of Guinea* (ed.

C.R. Beazely, 1937); G.R. Crone, *The Voyages of Cadamosto and Other Documents on Western Africa in the Second Half of the Fifteenth Century* (1937); and Anthony Luttrell, "Slavery and Slaving in the Portuguese Atlantic (to about 1500)", in Fyfe's *Transatlantic Slave Trade*. The early trade is treated in great depth in A.C. De C.M. Saunders, *A Social History of Black Slaves and Freemen in Portugal 1441-1555* (1982).

Among contemporary accounts of the trade by participants and travellers to Africa which deserve mention are: W. Bosman, *A New and Accurate Description of the Coast of Guinea* (1705); J.B. Labat, *Nouveau voyage aux isles de l'Amerique* (1722); W. Snelgrave, *A New Account of Some Parts of Guinea, and the Slave Trade* (1734); J. Atkins, *A Voyage to Guinea, Brazil and the West Indies* (1733); W. Smith, *A New Voyage to Guinea* (1744); L.F. Romer, *Tilforladelig Efterrentning om Kysten Guinea* (1760); P.E. Isert, *Reise nach Guinea und den Caribaischen Insel in Columbian* (1788); J. Mathews, *A Voyage to the River Sierra Leone* (1788); A. Falconbridge, *An Account of the Slave Trade on the Coast of Africa* (1788); C.B. Wadstrom, *Observations on the Slave Trade* (1789); R. Norris, *Memoirs of the Reign of Bossa Ahadee, King of Dahomey* (1789); N. Owen, *Journal of a Slave-Dealer* (1930 ed.); C.D. Forde (ed.), *Efik Traders of Old Calabar* (1956); J. Newton, *The Journal of a Slave Trader* (1962 ed.); —, *Letters to a Wife* (1793); —, *An Authentic Narrative of. . . the Life of John Newton* (1782); J. Adams, *Sketches Taken during Ten Voyages to Africa* (1822); H. Crow, *Memoirs of a Slave Trader* (1830); and P. Labarthe, *Voyage au Sénégal pendant les Années 1784 et 1785* (1802). Abstracts from some of these are included in sources cited under Introduction, for example Donnan's *Documents*.

While accounts by European slave traders exist in large number, those by the African victims of the trade are less numerous. *The Life of Olaudah Equiano* (1837) is the fascinating autobiography of an Igbo who was kidnapped around 1756 and sold as a slave. Grant's *The Fortunate Slave* (1968) tells the story of Ayuba Suleiman Diallo from Bondu, who was kidnapped on the Gambia in 1730 and sold into slavery, but was subsequently returned. The experiences of some of the victims are also included in Curtin's *Africa Remembered*.

A large body of useful data was also collected by various Parliamentary Committees in England during the late eighteenth century: House of Commons Reports, V (1778-82) and IX (1790-92); *Minutes of the Evidence Taken Before Committees and Accounts and Reports*, 1789, xxiv, xxv and xxvi; *Minutes of the Evidence: Select Committee on the Slave Trade*, 1790, xiv, and 1790, xxx; *Abstracts of Muster Rolls*, 1790-91, xxiv, 1802, iv and viii, 1792, xxxv.

There are also studies that give detailed descriptions of the slave trade in the context of given geographical areas. The Upper Guinea Coast and Senegambia are admirably covered in W. Rodney, *A History of the Upper Guinea Coast* (1970), and in P.D. Curtin, *Economic Change in Pre-Colonial Africa: Senegambia in the Era of the Slave Trade* (1975). Works that touch upon the trade in the Gold Coast include W. Rodney, "Gold and Slaves on the Gold Coast", in *Transactions of the Historical Society of Ghana* (1969); M. Priestley, *West African Trade and Coast Society* (1969); K.Y. Daaku, *Trade and Politics on the Gold Coast* (1970); Sammy Tenkorang, "British Slave Trading Activities on the Gold and Slave Coasts of the Eighteenth Century", M.A. thesis, University of London, 1964; R. Law, *The Oyo Empire* (1977); and E. Reynolds, *Trade and Economic Change on the Gold Coast* (1974). The trade on the Bight of Benin is dealt with in I.A. Akinjogbin's *Dahomey and its Neighbours, 1708-1818* (1967). Useful discussions of the slave trade are contained in P. Manning, "Growth Despite Slavery and Taxes: The Bight of Benin, 1640-1960" (1978); — , *Slavery, Colonialism and Economic Growth in Dahomey* (1982); and in W. Peukert, *Der Atlantische Sklavenhandel von Dahomey* (1978). The Niger Delta is covered in K.O. Dike, *Trade and Politics of the Niger Delta* (1956); A.J.H. Latham, *Old Calabar* (1973); and D. Northrup, *Trade Without Rulers* (1978). On Angola, see D. Birmingham, *Trade and Conflict in Angola* (1966), and J.C. Miller, "The Slave Trade in Congo and Angola", in Kilson and Rotberg's *African Diaspora*. The trade in the Kongo area is examined in P. Martin, *The External Trade of the Loango Coast* (1972), and in R.W. Harms, *River of Wealth, River of Sorrow* (1981).

The slave trade of the various American and European countries is studied in works which include: M. Craton, *Sinews of Empire: A Short History of British Slavery* (1974); L.B. Rout, Jr., *The African Experience in Spanish America* (1976); R. Mellafe, *Negro Slavery in Latin America* (1971); S.E. Green-Pedersen, "The Scope and Structure of the Danish Slave Trade", in *Scandinavian Economic History Review* (1971); P. Duignan and C. Clendenen, *The United States and the African Slave Trade* (1963); A. Mackenzie-Grieve, *The Last Years of the English Slave Trade* (1941); G. Martin, *Histoire de l'esclavage dans les colonies françaises* (1948); U.B. Phillips, *American Negro Slavery* (1918); H.A. Wyndham, *The Atlantic and Slavery* (1935); G.E. Brooks, Jr., *Yankee Traders, Old Coasters and African Middlemen* (1970); P.C. Emmer, "The History of the Dutch Slave Trade: A Bibliographical Survey", in *Journal of Economic History* (1972); J. Postma, "The Dutch Slave Trade", in Minchinton and Emmer's *Atlantic Slave Trade*; —, "The Origin of African Slaves", in Engerman and Genovese's *Race and Slavery*.

Many European companies were organized to conduct the slave trade and there are some good histories of these. On the English, K.G. Davies's *The Royal African Company* (1957) is excellent. A. Ly's *La Compagnie du Sénégal* (1958) is a good study on the French.

The relationship of the disease environment and European choice of labour is covered in P.D. Curtin, "Epidemiology and the Slave Trade", in *Political Science Quarterly* (1968). The cost factor in the replacement of indentured servants in the British colonies by black slaves is discussed in R.N. Bean and R.P. Thomas, "The Adoption of Slave Labor in British America", in Gemery and Hogendorn, *Uncommon Market*. The roles of racial ideology and the choice of labour in the British colonies are treated in W.D. Jordan's *White over Black: American Attitudes towards the Negro, 1550-1812* (1968).

Despite abolition, the slave trade did not come to an end in the early nineteenth century. The East African trade, for example, reached a peak during the nineteenth century, and the best studies on this are E.A. Alpers, *The East African Slave Trade* (1967); — , "The French Slave Trade in East Africa", in *Cahiers d'études africaines* (1970); — , *Ivory and Slaves in East Central Africa* (1975). Other works of interest on the trade in Eastern Africa are R.W. Beachy, "The East African Ivory Trade in the Nineteenth Century", in *Journal of African History* (1967); — , *A Collection of Documents on the Slave Trade of Eastern Africa* (1976); M.D.W. Nwulia, *Britain and Slavery in East Africa* (1975); R. Coupland, *East Africa and its Invaders* (1938), and his *The Exploitation of East Africa 1856-1890: The Slave Trade and the Scramble* (1939).

The study of the nineteenth-century slave trade should be viewed in the context of the recent writing of D. Eltis, among whose incisive articles are "The Export of Slaves from Africa, 1821-1843", in *Journal of Economic History* (1977), "The Direction and Fluctuation of the Transatlantic Slave Trade", in Gemery and Hogendorn's *Uncommon Market*, and "The British Transatlantic Slave Trade after 1807", in *Maritime History* (1970).

1. The importance of the gold trade until the early part of the seventeenth century is receiving increasing emphasis. See R. Bean, "A Note on the Relative Importance of Slaves and Gold in West African Exports", in *Journal of African History*, XV, 3 (1974), pp.351-6.
2. See Reynolds, *Trade and Economic Change*, p.9; W. Rodney, "Gold and Slaves on the Gold Coast", *Transactions of the Historical Society of Ghana*, X (1969), pp.13-28.
3. R. Jobson, *The Golden Trade* (London, 1623), p.112.
4. See W. Rodney *How Europe Underdeveloped Africa* (London, 1972), p.90-1.

5. See Akinjogbin, *Dahomey and its Neighbours, 1708–1818* (London, 1967), p.77.

6. W. Smith, *A New Voyage* (London, 1744), p.171.

7. See B.K. Drake, "The Liverpool-African Voyage c.1790-1807, Commercial Problems", in Anstey and Hair, *Liverpool*, pp.126-56.

8. See Mannix and Cowley, *Black Cargoes* (New York, 1962), pp.131-52.

9. Newton, *Journal of a Slave Trader* (ed. Martin and Spurrell, London, 1962), p.xiv.

10. Ibid.

11. Barbot, in Churchill, *Collection of Voyages and Travels*, V (London, 1732), p.523.

12. See R. L. Stein, *The French Slave Trade* (Madison, 1979), p.73.

13. Daaku, *Trade and Economic Change on the Gold Coast* (Oxford, 1970), p.38.

14. Curtin, *Economic Change in Precolonial Africa*, pp.154-68.

15. See Barbot, *Collection of Voyages*, I, pp.577-8.

16. Northrup, *Trade Without Rulers*, pp.65-9, and P.E.H. Hair, "The Enslavement of Koelle's Informants", in *Journal of African History*, VI, 2 (1965), pp.193-203.

17. Barbot, *Collection of Voyages*, V, p.4.

18. Matthews, *A Voyage on the River Sierra-Leone on the Coast of Africa* (London, 1788), p.40.

19. Quoted in A. Benezet, *Some Historical Account of Guinea* (London, 1788), p.99.

20. Newton, *Journal*, p.109.

21. On the economic and political models of enslavement, see Curtin, *Economic Change*, pp.156-68.

22. See Northrup, *Trade Without Rulers*, pp.75-6; Reynolds, *Trade and Economic Change*, p.13; and Harms, *River of Wealth, River of Sorrow* (New Haven, 1981), p.37.

23. Barbot, *Collection of Voyages*, V, p.47.

24. Equiano, *The Life of Olaudah Equiano or Gustavus Vassa* (London, 1789), pp.31-2.

25. Bosman, *A New and Accurate Description of the Coast of Guinea* (London, 1705).

26. Matthews, *Voyage*, p.146.

27. Barbot, *Collection of Voyages*, V, p.47.

28. See "Dicky Sam", *Liverpool and Slavery* (London, 1884), pp.26-7.

29. Rodney, *History of the Upper Guinea Coast*, (Oxford, 1970), p.106.

30. Northrup, *Trade Without Rulers*, pp.69-73.

31. Ibid., p.107.

32. For a discussion of the slave supply mechanism, see P.E. Lovejoy and J.S. Hogendorn, "Slave Marketing in West Africa", in Gemery and Hogendorn, *Uncommon Market*, pp.213-35, and Mahdi Amadu, "The Delivery of Slaves from the Central Sudan to the Bight of Benin in the Eighteenth and Nineteenth Centuries", in ibid., pp.163-80.

33. See Peukert, *Atlantische Sklavenhandel*.

34. Latham, *Old Calabar*, p.38.

35. See particularly Northrup, *Trade Without Rulers*, pp.114-15.

36. See Birmingham, *Trade and Conflict*, pp.40-1, 60-1, 78-81, 85-6.

37. F. Moore, *Travels into the Inland Parts of Africa* (London, 1753), p.28.

38. Barbot, *Collection of Voyages*, V, p.326.

39. Mackenzie-Grieve, *The Last Years of the English Slave Trade* (London, 1941), p.80.

40. Owen, *Journal of a Slave Dealer* (London, 1930), p.85.

41. Newton, *Journal*, p.15.

42. Owen, *Journal*, p.76.

43. Great Britain, House of Commons, *Parliamentary Papers, Accounts and Papers*, 1789, XXVI (646), p.1, evidence of Captain Heatley.

44. See Anstey, *Atlantic Slave Trade*, p.20.

45. See Wyndham, *Atlantic and Slavery*, p.78.

46. Barbot, *Collection of Voyages*, V, p.43.

47. For detailed discussion on slave prices, see R. Bean, *The British Trans-Atlantic Slave Trade* (New York, 1975), Chapter IV, and Eltis, "The Transatlantic Slave Trade".

48. See Bean, *British Trans-Atlantic Trade*, pp.68-75.

49. See Eltis, "Transatlantic Slave Trade", p.240.

50. See M. Johnson, "The Ounce in Eighteenth-Century West African Trade", in *Journal of African History*, (1966), and Martin, *External Trade of the Loango Coast*, pp.107-8.

51. Newton, *Journal*, p.106.

52. Canot, *Captain Canot*, p.64.

53. Bosman, *New and Accurate Description*, p.340.

54. Newton, *Journal*, p.103; see also Klein, *Middle Passage*, pp.148-52, 243-7.

55. Atkins, *Voyage to Guinea*, p.179.

3: The Middle Passage (pp. 47-56)

Many works contain illuminating material relating to the journey to the New World. Klein's *Middle Passage* gives excellent information about many aspects. Useful data on the journey can be found in Donnan, *Documents*, Vol.2; Snelgrave, *New Account of . . . the Slave Trade*; Falconbridge, *Account of the Slave Trade*; T. Canot, *Captain Canot, or Twenty Years of an African Slaver* (1854); G. Williams, *History of the Liverpool Privateers and Letters of Marque with an Account of the Liverpool Slave Trade* (1897), and other contemporary accounts cited under Chapter 2. The Minutes of the Evidence contained in the Parliamentary Papers cited under Chapter 3 are also valuable.

The mortality of the Middle Passage is discussed in H. Klein, "Slave Mortality on British Ships, 1791-1797", in Anstey and Hair, *Liverpool*, and his "Shipping Patterns and Mortality in the African Slave Trade to Rio de Janeiro", in *Cahiers d'études africaines* (1975); H.S. Klein and S.L. Engerman, "Facteures de mortalité dans le trafic français d'esclaves au xviii siècle", in *Annales, économies, sociétés, civilisations* (1976); — , "A Note on Mortality in the French Slave Trade in the Eighteenth Century", in Gemery and Hogendorn, *Uncommon Market*; and J. Postma, "Mortality in the Dutch Slave Trade, 1675-1795", in ibid. A recent study that discusses the findings of the authors above and looks at statistical evidence on causality is J.C. Miller's "Mortality in the Atlantic Slave Trade", in *Journal of Interdisciplinary History* (1981).

1. See Canot, *Captain Canot*, p.70.
2. *Life of Olaudah Equiano*, pp.43-4.
3. John Weskett, *A Complete Digest of the Laws, Theory and Practice of Insurance* (London, 1781), p.525.
4. Newton, *Journal*, p.104.
5. On slave mortality, see Klein, *Middle Passage*, pp.64-7, 73-94; Curtin, *Census*, pp.275-86; Klein, "Slave Mortality on British Ships, 1791-1797", in Anstey and Hair, *Liverpool*; Miller, "Mortality in the Atlantic Slave Trade", in *Journal of Interdisciplinary History* (1981); Postma, "Mortality in the Dutch Slave Trade", in Gemery and Hogendorn, *Uncommon Market*, pp.239-60; and Klein and Engerman, "Note on Mortality in the French Slave Trade", in ibid., pp.261-72.
6. See Lamb, "Volume and Tonnage of the Liverpool Slave Trade 1772-1807".
7. E. Van den Boogart and P.C. Emmer, "The Dutch Participation in the Atlantic Slave Trade 1596-1650", in Gemery and Hogendorn, *Uncommon Market*, pp.365-8.

4: Demand, Supply and Distribution (pp. 57-73)

The expansion of Europe which brought Europeans to Africa and the Americas and also introduced plantation slavery to these areas are covered by a large body of literature. I. Wallerstein has provided stimulating books and articles on the subject, including *The Modern World System: Capitalist Agriculture and the Origins of the European World-Economy in the Sixteenth Century* (1974); "The Three Stages of African Involvement in the World Economy", in P.C.W. Gutkind and I. Wallerstein (eds.), *The Political Economy of Contemporary Africa* (1976), and "Africa in a Capitalist World", in *Issue* (1973). Other excellent works on European expansion include P. Channu, *L'expansion européene du xiiie au xve siècle* (1969); F. Mauro, *Étude économique sur l'expansion portugaise* (1970); — , *Portugal et l'Atlantique au xviie siècle: Etude économique* (1970); V. Magalhaes-Godinho, *L'économie de l'empire portugais* (1969); C.R. Boxer, *The Portuguese Seaborne Empire* (1969); — , *Salvador de Sa and the Struggle for Brazil and Angola* (1952), and — , *The Dutch in Brazil, 1624-1654* (1957).

The labour needs which led to the rise of slavery are studied in terms of their close relation to Amerindian demography in: N. Sanchez-Albornoz, *The Population of Latin America* (1974), and A. Rosenblat, *La población indígena y el mestizaje en América* (1954). Spanish and Portuguese policy and labour activities are covered in C.O. Sauer, *The Early Spanish Main* (1969); S.B. Schwartz, "Indian Labor and the New World Plantations: European Demands and Indian Responses in Northeast Brazil", in *American Historical Review* (1978); J.H. Elliott, *Imperial Spain 1470-1716* (1963); L. Hanke, *The Spanish Struggle for Justice in the Conquest of Latin America* (1949); and L.B. Simpson, *The Encomienda in New Spain* (1950).

Important studies explaining the demand and supply of slaves include: N. Deerr, *A History of Sugar* (2 vols, 1949-50); R.S. Dunn, *Sugar and Slaves* (1972): F.P. Bowser, *The African Slave in Colonial Peru, 1524-1650* (1974); P.H. Wood, *Black Majority* (1974); S.J. Stein, *Vassouras, a Brazilian Coffee County, 1850-1900* (1957); and A.J.R. Russell-Wood, *The Black Man in Slavery and Freedom in Colonial Brazil* (1982). A superb work on the French slave trade is R.L. Stein, *The French Slave Trade in the Eighteenth Century* (1979), and the Spanish trade is studied in C. Palmer, *Human Cargoes: The British Slave Trade to Spanish America* (1981).

1. On the origins of the Atlantic system and the transfer of the plantation system from the Mediterranean area to the coasts of the Atlantic Ocean, see Verlinden, *Les origines de la civilisation Atlantique* (Paris, 1956), and *Précédents méditerrané de la colonie en Amerique* (Mexico, 1954).

2. P.E. Lovejoy, "The Volume of the Atlantic Slave Trade: A Synthesis", in *Journal of African History* 23 (1982), 473-501; see also *Transformations in Slavery*, Chapter 3.

3. See Wallerstein, "Africa in the Capitalist World", in *Issue*, 3 (1973), 1-11; *The Modern World System* (New York, 1974), and "The Three Stages of African Involvement in the World Economy", in Gutkind and Wallerstein, *Political Economy of Contemporary Africa* (Beverly Hills, 1976).

4. See Bartolome Bennassar, *The Spanish Character* (Berkeley, 1979), pp. 106-17.

5. Curtin, *Census*, pp.17-21.

6. See Klein, *Middle Passage*, p.3; also Sanchez-Albornoz, *The Population of Latin America* (Berkeley, 1974).

7. See G. Cespedes, *Latin America, The Early Years* (New York, 1974), pp. 49-52.

8. On the *asiento*, see Palmer, *Human Cargoes* (Chicago, 1981); Rout, *The African Experience in Spanish America* (London, 1976), pp. 37-66, and Deerr, *A History of Sugar*, 2 (London, 1949-50), p. 263.

9. See Boxer, *Salvador de Sa and the Struggle for Brazil and Angola* (London, 1952), p. 231.

10. Curtin, *Census*, pp. 21-5, and Palmer, *Human Cargoes*, p. 111.

11. See M.M. Fraginals, H.S. Klein and S.L. Engerman, "The Level and Structure of Slave Prices on Cuban Plantations in the Mid-Nineteenth Century", in *American Historical Review*, 88, 5 (1983), p. 1205.

12. See Deerr, *Sugar*, p. 260.

13. See Celso Furtado, *The Economic Growth of Brazil* (Berkeley, 1971).

14. On the Dutch in West Africa, see J.D. Fage, *A History of West Africa* (Cambridge, 1969), pp. 68-70.

15. See C.R. Boxer, *The Golden Age of Brazil, 1695-1750* (Berkeley, 1969), and A.J.R. Russell-Wood, "Technology and Society: The Impact of Gold Mining on the Institution of Slavery in Portuguese America", in *Journal of Economic History*, xv (1977), pp. 59-83.

16. See R. Davis, *Rise of the Atlantic Economies* (Ithaca, 1973), ch. 15.

17. For the British West Indies, see Dunn, *Sugar and Slaves* (Chapel Hill, 1972), and F.W. Pitman, *The Development of the British West Indies* (Hamden, 1967).

18. See Dunn, *Sugar and Slaves*, pp. 84-116.
19. See Bean and Thomas, "The Adoption of Slave Labor in British America", in Gemery and Hogendorn, *Uncommon Market*, pp. 377-98.
20. See Dunn, *Sugar and Slaves*, pp. 149-87.
21. See ibid., pp. 230 and 234.
22. See Stein, *French Slave Trade*, p. 200.
23. See J. Postma, "A Quantitative Assessment of the Dutch Slave Trade", in Engerman and Genovese, *Race and Slavery*, pp. 33-49.
24. On the trade to British North America, see Tommy Todd Hamm, "The American Slave Trade with Africa, 1620-1807", unpublished doctoral thesis, Indiana University, 1975.
25. Quoted in Donnan, *Documents*, IV, p. 92.
26. See R.W. Fogel and S.L. Engerman, *Time on the Cross* (Boston, 1974), p.14.

5: The End of Black Slavery (pp. 74-92)

Three excellent studies on the abolition issue are D. Eltis and J. Walvin, *The Abolition of the Atlantic Slave Trade* (1981), D.H. Porter, *The Abolition of the Slave Trade in England* (1970), and R. Anstey, *The Atlantic Slave Trade and British Abolition* (1975). Some of the early works on the subject came soon after abolition was effected. T. Clarkson, *History of . . . the Abolition of the African Slave-Trade by the British Parliament* (1808), presents abolition as a contest between good and righteous people and wicked and evil people. Sir R. Coupland's *The British Anti-Slavery Movement* (1935) emphasized the movement's religious and humanitarian aspects. Other writers who stressed the humanitarian aspect include F.J. Klingberg, *The Anti-Slavery Movement in England* (1926), C.M. Innes, *England and Slavery* (1934), and L.J. Ragatz, *The Fall of the Planter Class in the British Caribbean* (1928). The decline thesis posited by Ragatz lent itself to an economic interpretation, and two works in particular that espouse brilliant economic expositions are E. Williams, *Capitalism and Slavery* (1944), and F. Hochstetter, *Die wirtschaftlichen und politischen Motive für die Abschaffung des britischen Sklavenhandels* (1905).

The intellectual origins of the anti-slavery movement are covered superbly in D.B. Davis, *The Problem of Slavery in Western Culture* (1966). Other works dealing with this theme include: W. Sypher, *Guinea's Captive Kings: British Anti-Slavery Literature of the XVIII Century* (1942); F.T.H. Fletcher, *Montesquieu and English Politics* (1939); E.E. Seeber, *Anti-Slavery Opinion in France* (1937); F.O. Shyllon, *Black Slaves in Britain* (1974).

The literature on abolition of the slave trade often concentrates on the British initiatives, but other nations involved in the trade also legislated against it. Abolition in the United States is covered in W.E.B. Du Bois, *The Suppression of the African Slave-Trade to the United States of America* (1896); well researched and well written, this work has stood the test of time remarkably well. The abolition of the trade by Denmark, the first European nation to do so, is covered in G. Norregard, *Danish Settlements in West Africa* (1966); S.E. Green-Pedersen, "The Economic Considerations behind the Danish Abolition of the Negro Slave Trade", in Gemery and Hogendorn's *Uncommon Market*, pp.399-418. Spanish abolition is admirably covered in D. Murray, *Odious Commerce: Britain, Spain and the Abolition of the Cuban Slave Trade* (1980).

The contribution of British missionaries to the abolition movement is dealt with by S. Jakobsson in *Am I not a Man and a Brother* (1972).

There is a rich body of literature on the abolition of slavery itself, but this book's focus on the abolition of the slave trade precludes detailed mention of such works. For the relation between the ending of the slave trade and European colonization, see S. Miers, *Britain and the Ending of the Slave Trade* (1975).

1. R. and S. Wilberforce, *Life of William Wilberforce* (5 vols, London, 1838), II, p.7.
2. Lecky, *A History of European Morals*, I (London, 1869), p.153.
3. Clarkson, *History of the Rise, Progress and Accomplishment of the Abolition of the African Slave-Trade* (London, 1808), vol. 2, pp.280-81.
4. See Ragatz, *Fall of the Planter Class in the British Caribbean* (New York, 1929).
5. Williams, *Capitalism and Slavery*, p.169
6. Ibid., p.136.
7. See S. Drescher, *Econocide, British Slavery in the Era of Abolition* (Pittsburgh, 1977).
8. Ibid., pp.16-25.
9. Ibid., pp.25-32.
10. On anti-slavery and ideology, see Davis, *The Problem of Slavery in the Age of Revolution* (Ithaca, 1975), p.14.
11. On slave revolts, see H. Aptheker, "American Negro Slave Revolts", in *Science and Society*, I (1937), pp.512-38, — *Negro Slave Revolts in the United States* (New York, 1939); J.C. Caroll, *Slave Insurrect in the United States* (Boston, 1938); E.D. Genovese, *From Rebellic Revolution: Afro-American Slave Revolts in the Making of Modern World* (Baton Rouge, 1979); C.L.R. James, *The B Jacobins* (London, 1938).

12. See Davis, *Problem of Slavery, passim*. See also Du Bois, *Suppression of the African Slave Trade*.

13. See Shyllon, *Black Slaves in Britain*, pp.18-21.

14. Ibid., pp.109-10.

15. See Mannix and Cowley, *Black Cargoes*, p.176.

16. Quoted in Anstey, *Atlantic Slave Trade*, p.255.

17. See D.H. Porter, *The Abolition of the Slave Trade in England* (Hamden, 1970), pp.36-7.

18. See Anstey, *Atlantic Slave Trade*, pp.319-42.

19. Quoted in ibid., p.379.

20. Ibid., p.407.

21. See C. Lloyd, *The Navy and the Slave Trade* (London, 1968), pp.3-12.

22. On Denmark see S.E. Green-Pederson, "History of the Danish Negro Slave Trade", pp.196-220, and Norregard, *Danish Settlements in West Africa*, pp.183-4. On the Dutch, see P. Emmer, "Anti-Slavery and the Dutch: Abolition without Reform", in Bolt and Drescher, *Anti-Slavery, Religion and Reform*, pp.80-98. On France, see S. Drescher, "Two Variants of Anti-Slavery; Religious Organization and Social Mobilization in Britain and France, 1780-1870", in ibid., pp.43-63.

23. See Lloyd, *Navy and the Slave Trade*, pp.39-60.

24. Ibid., p.26.

25. Ibid., pp.45-60.

26. On Brazilian abolition of slavery, see Robert Brent Toplin, *The Abolition of Slavery in Brazil* (New York, 1972), and R. Conrad, *The Destruction of Brazilian Slavery* (Berkeley, 1972). On abolition of slavery in Cuba, see F.W. Knight, *Slave Society in Cuba during the Nineteenth Century* (Madison, 1970), pp.137-78; A.F. Corwin, *Spain and the Abolition of Slavery in Cuba* (Austin, 1967), and Murray, *Odious Commerce*.

27. See L. Bethell, *Abolition of the Brazilian Slave Trade*.

28. See Knight, *Slave Society in Cuba*, pp.154-78.

29. Ibid., pp.137-53.

30. Ibid., pp.172-7.

31. Ibid.

32. See Lloyd, *Navy and the Slave Trade*, pp. 149-62.

33. See J.U.J. Asiegbu, *Slavery and Politics of Liberation* (New York, 1969).

34. On the American Colonization Society, see P.J. Standenraus, *American Colonization Movement, 1816-1865* (New York, 1961).

35. For further information on American anti-slavery, see Gilbert Hobbes Barnes, *The Antislavery Impulse* (Gloucester, 1933), and Ronald G. Walters, *The Antislavery Appeal* (Baltimore, 1977).

6: The Legacy of the Slave Trade in Africa (pp. 93-106)

The best summary of the impact of the slave trade on Africa is in A.G. Hopkins, *An Economic History of West Africa* (1973). W. Rodney's *How Europe Underdeveloped Africa* (1972) also contains excellent material on this. Other useful books are Northrup, *Trade Without Rulers;* Daaku, *Trade and Politics on the Gold Coast*; G.N. Uzoigwe, "The Slave Trade and African Societies", in *Transactions of the Historical Society of Ghana* (1973); Peukert, *Der Atlantische Sklavenhandel*; P. Manning, "Contours of Slavery and Social Change in Africa", in *American Historical Review* (1983); and J.E. Inikori, *Forced Migration: The Impact of the Export Trade on African Societies* (1982).

The relationship between the slave trade and population is discussed by J.D. Fage, "The Effect of the Export Trade on African Populations", in R.P. Moss and R.J.A. Rathbone (eds.), *The Population Factor in African Society* (1975), pp.15-23; C. Fyfe, "A Brief Note on the Demographic Effects of the Trans-Atlantic Slave Trade on West Africa", in *African Historical Demography* (1977); M. Johnson, "Census, Map and Guesstimate: The Past Population of the Accra Region", in *African Historical Demography*; and R.W. Beachy, "Some Observations on the Volume of the Slave Trade on Eastern Africa in the Nineteenth Century", in *African Historical Demography*. Miers, *Britain and the Ending of the Slave Trade*, touches upon the relationship between the slave trade, its abolition and the acquisition of colonies.

1. Rodney, *How Europe Underdeveloped Africa*, p.115.
2. Uzoigwe, "The Slave Trade and African Societies", in *Transactions of the Historical Society of Ghana*, Vol. 14 (1973), pp.187-212.
3. See E. Boserup, *The Conditions of Agricultural Growth* (London, 1965).
4. Curtin, *Census*, pp. 270-1.
5. On slave exports from Senegambia see Curtin, *Census*, pp.108, 152-3, and *Economic Change in Precolonial Africa*, pp.156-8.
6. On Upper Guinea slave exports, see Curtin, *Census*, pp.153-96.
7. On the Gold Coast, see ibid., pp.154-5, 226-7.
8. On the Windward Coast, see ibid., pp.152-3, and A. Jones and M. Johnson, "Slaves from the Windward Coast", in *Journal of African History*, 21, I (1980), pp.17-34.

9. On exports from the Bight of Benin, see Curtin, *Census*, pp.227, and Manning, "Slave Trade in the Bight of Benin", in Gemery and Hogendorn, *Uncommon Market*, pp.107-41.

10. On slave exports from the Niger Delta, see Curtin, *Census*, pp.128-30, and Northrup, *Trade Without Rulers*, pp.54-8.

11. See J.C. Miller, "Legal Portuguese Slaving from Angola: Some Preliminary Indications of Volume and Direction, 1760-1830", in *Revue Français d'Histoire d'Outre-Mer*, lx, nos.226-7 (1975), pp.135-76, and Birmingham, *Trade and Conflict*

12. See P. Manning, *Slavery, Colonialism and Economic Growth in Dahomey* (Cambridge, 1982), and "Growth Despite Slavery and Taxes: The Bight of Benin, 1640-1960".

13. See Johnson, "Census, Map and Guesstimate: The Past Population of the Accra Region", in *African Historical Demography*, Centre of African Studies (Edinburgh University), pp.272-93.

14. J. Thornton, "The Slave Trade in Eighteenth-Century Angola: Effects on Demographic Structures", in *Canadian Journal of African Studies*, 14 (1980), pp.421-2.

15. See M. Johnson, "Technology, Competition, and African Crafts", in C. Dewey and A.G. Hopkins, *The Imperial Impact: Studies in the Economic History of Africa and India* (London, 1978), pp.259-69.

16. See H.A. Gemery and J.S. Hogendorn, "Technological Change, Slavery and the Slave Trade", ibid., pp.243-58.

17. Quoted in Daaku, *Trade and Politics*, p.152.

18. See W.A. Richards, "The Import of Firearms into West Africa in the Eighteenth Century", in *Journal of African Studies*, 21, no.1 (1980), pp.43-59.

19. Northrup, *Trade Without Rulers*, pp.175-96.

20. See Reynolds, "Agricultural Adjustment on the Gold Coast after the End of the Slave Trade, 1807-14", in *Agricultural History*, xiv, 4 (1973), pp.308-18.

21. See Peukert, *Der Atlantische Sklavenhandel von Dahomey*.

22. See J. Vansina, *Kingdoms of the Savanna* (Madison, 1968), pp.37-69, and Davidson, *Black Mother*, pp.115-62.

23. See Vansina, *Kingdoms of the Savanna*, pp.52-3.

24. Ibid., p.52.

25. On Benin, see A. Ryder, *Benin and the Europeans, 1485-1896* (London, 1969).

26. See Northrup, *Trade Without Rulers*, pp.114-45.

27. See M.A. Klein, "Slavery and the Slave Trade and Legitimate Commerce in Late Nineteenth-Century Africa", in *Études d'Histoire Africaine*, 2 (1971), pp.5-28.

7: Impact on the Americas (pp. 107-27)

A useful work that places the economic impact of the slave trade within the context of the Atlantic trade is R. Davis, *The Rise of the Atlantic Economies* (1973); and Williams's *Capitalism and Slavery* still has value, despite having been severely criticized. Criticisms levelled against Williams and in connection with the profitability of the trade have come from G.R. Mellor, *British Imperial Trusteeship* (1950); R.T. Anstey, "Capitalism and Slavery: A Critique", in *Economic History Review* (1968), — , "The Volume and Profitability of the British Slave Trade", in Engerman and Genovese, *Race and Slavery*,; and S.L. Engerman, "The Slave Trade and British Capital Formation in the Eighteenth Century: A Comment on the Williams Thesis", in *Business History Review* (1972). The view has also been expressed that the whole of the British colonial enterprise was unprofitable in R.P. Thomas, "The Sugar Colonies of the Old Empire, Profit or Loss for Great Britain?", in *Economic History Review* (1968); D.P. Richardson, "Profits in the Eighteenth-Century British Slave Trade: The Accounts of William Davenport of Liverpool", in Anstey and Hair, *Liverpool*, and — , "Profitability in the Bristol-Liverpool Slave Trade", in Minchinton and Emmer, *Atlantic Slave Trade*. R. Pares, *A West Indian Fortune* (1956), provides an account of the economic experience of one family on the island of Nevis. The works of Boxer, cited above, also provide some economic insight. Rodney's *How Europe Underdeveloped Africa* also merits attention and F.W. Pitman's *The Development of the British West Indies* (1967) is still valuable. Other useful works that touch upon the profitability of the slave trade include J. Meyer, *L'armement nantais dans la deuxième moitié du XVIII siècle* (1969); P. Viles, "The Slaving Interest of the Atlantic Ports, 1763-1792", in *French Historical Studies* (1972); R. Stein, "The Profitability of the Nantes Slave Trade", in *Journal of Economic History* (1975); and W.S. Unger, "Bijdraen tot de geschiedenis", in *Economisch Historisch Jaarboek* (1958).

Curtin's *Atlantic Slave Trade*, Klein's *Middle Passage* and Lovejoy's "The Volume of the Atlantic Slave Trade: A Synthesis", in *Journal of African Studies* (1982), provide a good basis for study of the demographic impact of the trade. Sanchez-Albornoz, *The Population of Latin America*, also gives some useful data.

A large number of serious books deal with the cultural impact of Africans on the Americas and on the subject of African retentions and the transfer of African culture: S.W. Mintz and R. Price (eds.), *An Anthropolo-*

gical Approach to the Afro-American Past: A Caribbean Perspective (1976), provides a stimulating evaluation. R. Bastide's *African Civilisations in the New World* is a comprehensive study. J.W. Blassingame, *The Slave Community: Plantation Life in the Antebellum South* (1972), utilizes material from Black sources in a fascinating analysis of the Black community in the United States. E. Genovese, *Roll, Jordan, Roll: The World the Slaves Made* (1974), is a superb work that should not be missed. O. Patterson, *The Sociology of Slavery* (1969), gives an excellent sociological examination of slave society in Jamaica. African cultural survivals are also studied in M.J. Herskovits, *The Myth of the Negro Past* (1958); E. Franklin Frazier, *The Negro in the United States* (1949); J.J. Williams, *Voodoos and Obeas* (1964); and A.J. Raboteau, *Slave Religion* (1978). Black family life is masterfully treated in H.G. Gutman, *The Black Family in Slavery and Freedom* (1976).

Slavery and the slave trade have also generated prejudice and racism and a useful starting point for studying this is G.W. Allport's *Race Questions and the Negro* (1958), and J. La Farge, *Race Questions and the Negro* (1945). Among major works on racism's momentous connections with slavery are Jordan's *White Over Black*; C.N. Degler, *Neither Black Nor White* (1971); H. Hoetink, *Slavery and Race Relations in the Americas* (1973); M. Mörner, *Race Mixture in the History of Latin America* (1967); F. Fernandes, *The Negro in Brazilian Society* (1971); G.M. Fredrickson, *The Black Image in the White Mind: The Debate on Afro-American Character and Destiny 1817-1914* (1971).

British attitudes towards Black people in the seventeenth to nineteenth centuries are reflected in such studies as A.J. Barker, *The African Link* (1978), and P.D. Curtin, *Image of Africa* (1956).

The global impact of the trade receive attention in J. Harris, *Global Dimensions of the African Diaspora* (1982), and V.B. Thompson, *The Making of the African Diaspora in the Americas* (1984).

1. See D.C. Coleman, *Revisions in Mercantilism* (London, 1969).
2. Quoted in Harry N. Scheiber, Harold G. Vater and Harold U. Faulkner, *American Economic History* (New York, 1976), pp.59-60.
3. See Williams, *Capitalism and Slavery*, pp.98-107.
4. M. Postlethwayt, *The African Trade, the Great Pillar and Support of the British Plantation Trade in North America* (London, 1745), p.4.
5. J. Campbell, *Candid and Impartial Observations on the Nature of the Sugar Trade* (London, 1763), pp.25-6.
6. Namier, *The Structure of Politics at the Accession of George III* (London, 1929), I, p.210.
7. Williams, *Capitalism and Slavery*, p.36.
8. Anstey, *Atlantic Slave Trade*, p.47.

9. Richardson, "Profitability in the Bristol-Liverpool Slave Trade", in Minchinton and Emmer, *Atlantic Slave Trade*, pp.301-8.
10. The calculation of profits for the French slave trade included government subsidies. For a comprehensive history, see Stein, *French Slave Trade*.
11. See Canot, *Twenty Years*, pp.68-9.
12. See Eltis, *Transatlantic Slave Trade*, p.243.
13. See W.E. Minchinton, "The Triangular Trade Revisited", in Gemery and Hogendorn, *Uncommon Market*, pp.331-52, B.K. Drake, "Continuity and Flexibility in Liverpool's Trade with Africa and the Caribbean", in *Business History*, 18 (1976), pp.85-97, and Williams, *Capitalism and Slavery*, pp.51-2.
14. See M. Morner (ed.), *Race and Class in Latin American History* (New York, 1970), pp.45-8; Rout, *African Experience in Spanish America*, pp.205-14, 278-380.
15. Mörner, *Race and Class* (Boston, 1970), pp.214-15.
16. See Raboteau, *Slave Religion*; Herskovits, *Myth of the Negro Past*, pp.277-360.
17. See Bastide, *African Civilisations in the New World* (London, 1971), p.8.
18. H. Roach, *Black American Music: Past and Present*, (New York, Crescendo, 1973), p.34.
19. P. Oliver, *Savannah Syncopators: African Retentions of the Blues* (Studio Vista, London, 1970), p.58.
20. J.M. Chernoff, *African Rhythm and African Sensibility: Aesthetics and Social Action in African Musical Idioms* (Chicago and London, 1979), p.73.
21. Roach, *Black American Music*, p.71.
22. Henry H. Mitchell, *The Recovery of Preaching* (New York, 1977), p.84.
23. See Helen Mendes, *The African Heritage Cookbook* (New York, 1971), Evan Jones, *American Food* (New York, 1975).
24. W.J. Cash, *The Mind of the South* (New York, 1941), p.87.
25. See Gutman, *The Black Family in Slavery and Freedom*.
26. Blassingame, *The Slave Community* (New York, 1979), p.151.
27. Bernard Lewis, "The African Diaspora and Civilization of Islam", in Kilson and Rotberg, *African Diaspora*, p.44.
28. W. Rodney, "Africa in Europe and the Americas", in *Cambridge History of Africa*, Vol.4 (ed. Richard Gray), p.582.
29. Boxer, *Race Relations*, p.46.
30. Ibid., pp.129-30.
31. Fernandes, *The Negro in Brazilian Society* (New York, 1971), p.133.
32. A. Haley, *Roots* (New York, 1977).

Select Bibliography

ABRAHAM, W.E.: *The Mind of Africa* (London, Weidenfeld & Nicolson, 1962).

ABRAHAMS, Roger D., and SZWED, John F.: *After Africa: Extracts from British travel accounts and journals of the 17th, 18th and 19th centuries concerning the slaves, their manners and customs in the British West Indies* (Cambridge and London, Harvard University Press, 1983).

ADAMS, J.: *Sketches Taken during Ten Voyages to Africa between the Years 1786 and 1800* (London, Hurst, Robinson Co., 1822).

ADAMSON, Alan H.: *Sugar Without Slaves: The Political Economy of British Guiana, 1838–1904* (New Haven, Yale University Press, 1972).

AFIGBO, A.E.: "The Eclipse of the Aro Slave Oligarchy of South-Eastern Nigeria", *Journal of the Historical Society of Nigeria*, 6 (1971), 3–24.

AFRICAN MERCHANT, An: *A Treatise Upon the Trade From Great Britain to Africa, Humbly Recommended to the Attention of Government* (London, 1772).

AIMES, Hubert H.S.: *A History of Slavery in Cuba, 1511–1868* (New York, Putnam, 1907).

AKINJOGBIN, I.A.: *Dahomey and its Neighbours, 1708–1818* (Cambridge, Cambridge University Press, 1967).

ALLPORT, Gordon W.: *The Race Questions and the Negro* (New York, 1958).

ALAGOA, E.J.: "Long-distance Trade and States in the Niger Delta", *Journal of African History*, 11(1970), 319–29.

——: "The Development of Institutions in the States of the Eastern Niger Delta", *Journal of African History*, 12 (1971), 269–78.

ALPERS, Edward A.: *The East African Slave Trade* (Historical Association of Tanzania Paper, No.3, Nairobi, 1967).

——: "The French Slave Trade in East Africa, 1721–1810", *Cahiers d'Études Africaines*, 10 (1970), 80–124.

——: *Ivory and Slaves in East Central Africa: Changing Patterns of International Trade to the Late Nineteenth Century* (Berkeley, University of California Press, 1975).

ANSTEY Roger T.: "Capitalism and Slavery: A Critique", *Economic History Review*, 21 (1968), 307–20.

——: "The Volume and Profitability of the British Slave Trade, 1761–1807", in Engerman and Genovese, *Race and Slavery* (1975), 3–31.

——: *The Atlantic Slave Trade and British Abolition, 1760–1810* (London, Macmillan, 1975; Atlantic Highlands, NJ, Humanities Press, 1975).

——: "The British Slave Trade, 1751–1807", *Journal of African History*, 17 (1976), 606–7.

——: "The Volume of the North American Slave-Carrying Trade from Africa, 1761–1810", in Minchinton and Emmer, *Atlantic Slave Trade* (1976), 47–66.

——, and HAIR, P.E.H. (eds): *Liverpool: The African Slave Trade and Abolition. Essays to illustrate current knowledge and research* (Historic Society of Lancashire and Cheshire, occasional series, II, 1976).

APTHEKER, Herbert: *Negro Slave Revolts in the United States, 1526–1860* (New York, Columbia University Press, 1939).

ASIEGBU, Johnson U.J.: *Slavery and the Politics of Liberation, 1787–1861: A study of liberated African emigration and British anti-slavery policy* (New York, Africana Publishing Co., 1969).

ASTLEY: *A New General Collection of Voyages and Travels* (4 vols, London, 1745–7).

ATKINS, John: *A voyage to Guinea, Brasil and the West-Indies* (London, C. Ward and R. Chandler, 1735).

AUSTEN, Ralph A.: "The Abolition of the Overseas Slave Trade: A Distorted Theme in West African History", *Journal of the Historical Society of Nigeria*, 5 (1970), 257–74.

——: "The Trans-Saharan Slave Trade: A Tentative Census", in Gemery and Hogendorn, *Uncommon Market* (1979), 23–76.

——, and SMITH, W.D.: "Images of Africa and British Slave Trade Abolition: The Transition to an Imperialist Ideology, 1787–1807", *African Historical Studies*, II (1969), 69–83.

BANDINEL, James: *Some Account of the Trade in Slaves from Africa* (London, Longman, 1842).

BARBOT, John: *A Description of the Coasts of North and South Guinea*, in Churchill, *Collection of Voyages* (1732).

BARKER, Anthony J.: *The African Link: British Attitudes to the Negro in the Seventeenth and Eighteenth Centuries* (London, Frank Cass, 1978).

BASTIDE, Roger: *African Civilisations in the New World (Les Amériques Noires: les civilisations africaines dans le nouveau monde)* Paris, Payot, 1967: trans. Peter Green, London, Hurst, 1971; New York, Harper & Row, 1972).

BEACHY, R.W.A.: "The East African Ivory Trade in the Nineteenth Century", *Journal of African History*, 8 (1967), 268–90.

——: *A Collection of Documents on the Slave Trade of Eastern Africa*

(London, Rex Collings, 1976).

——: "Some Observations on the Volume of the Slave Trade in Eastern Africa in the Nineteenth Century", *African Historical Demography*.

BEAN, Richard: "A Note on the Relative Importance of Slaves and Gold in West African Exports", *Journal of African History*, 15 (1974), 351–6.

——: *The British Trans-Atlantic Slave Trade, 1650–1775* (New York, Arno Press, 1975).

——, and THOMAS, Robert P.: "The Adoption of Slave Labor in British America", in Gemery and Hogendorn, *Uncommon Market* (1979), 377–98.

BEBEY, Francis: *African Music: A People's Art* (London, Harrap, 1975; New York, L. Hill, 1975).

BENEZET, Anthony: *Observations on the Enslaving, Importing and Purchasing of Negroes with some Advice thereon Extracted from the Yearly Meeting Epistle of London for the Present Year* (Society of Friends, Germantown, 1759).

——: *A Caution and Warning to Great Britain and her Colonies, in a Short Representation of the Calamitous State of the Enslaved Negroes in the British Dominions* (London, James Phillips, 1784).

——: *Some Historical Account of Guinea, Its Situation, Produce and the General Disposition of its Inhabitants. With An Inquiry into the Rise and Progress of the Slave-Trade, its Nature and lamentable Effects* (Philadelphia, 1771; London, 1788).

BETHEL, Leslie: "The Mixed Commissions for the Suppression of the Transatlantic Slave Trade in the Nineteenth Century", *Journal of African History*, 7 (1966), 79–93.

——: *The Abolition of the Brazilian Slave Trade: Britain, Brazil and the Slave Trade Question, 1807–1869* (Cambridge University Press, 1970).

BIRMINGHAM, David: *Trade and Conflict in Angola: The Mbundu and their neighbours under the influence of the Portuguese, 1483–1790* (Oxford, Clarendon Press, 1966).

BLAKE, John W.: *European Beginnings in West Africa, 1454–1578* (New York, 1937).

BLASSINGAME, John W.: *The Slave Community: Plantation Life in the Antebellum South* (New York, Oxford University Press, 1973).

BOAHEN, A. Adu: *Britain, the Sahara, and the Western Sudan, 1788–1861* (Oxford, 1964).

BOLT, Christine: *The Anti-Slavery Movement and Reconstruction* (Oxford, Oxford University Press, 1969).

——, and DRESCHER, Seymour: *Anti-Slavery, Religion and Reform* (London, Dawson, 1980).

BOOTH, Alan R.: "The United States African Squadron, 1843–1861", *Boston University Papers in African History*, I (1964), 79–117.

BOSERUP, Ester: *The Conditions of Agricultural Growth: The economics of agrarian change under population pressure* (Chicago, Aldine Publishing Co., 1965).

BOSMAN, Willem: *A New and Accurate Description of the Coast of Guinea* (London, J. Knapton, 1705; 2nd edn 1721).

BOUTILLIER, J-L.: "Les captifs en A.O.F., 1903–1905", *Bulletin de l'IFAN*, series B, 30, 2:513–35.

BOVILL, E.W.: *The Golden Trade of the Moors* (London, Oxford University Press, 1968).

BOWSER, Frederick P.: *The African Slave in Colonial Peru, 1524–1560* (Stanford, Stanford University Press, 1974).

BOXER, C.R.: *Salvador de Sa and the Struggle for Brazil and Angola, 1602–1686* (London, University of London Press, 1952).

——: *The Dutch in Brazil, 1624–1654* (Oxford, Clarendon Press, 1957).

——: *The Portuguese Seaborne Empire* (London, 1969; New York, Knopf, 1969).

BRATHWAITE, Edward Kamau: *The Folk Culture of the Slaves in Jamaica* (London and Port of Spain, New Beacon Books, 1981).

BROOKS, George E., Jr.: *Yankee Traders, Old Coasters and African Middlemen: A History of American Legitimate Trade with West Africa in the Nineteenth Century* (Boston, Boston University Press, 1970).

BRORON, George W.: "The Origin of Abolition in Santo Domingo", *Journal of Negro History*, 7 (1922), 365-76.

BUXTON, Thomas Fowell: *The African Slave Trade and its Remedy* (London, John Murray, 2nd edn 1840).

CADAMOSTO, A. Da: *The Voyages of Cadamosto* (Paris, 1853; trans. G. R. Crone, London, Hakluyt Society, 1937).

CAMERON, V.L.: "Slavery in Africa: The Disease and the Remedy", *National Review*, 10, 260–9.

CANOT, Theodore: *Captain Canot, or Twenty Years of an African Slaver* (London, Richard Bentley, 1854).

CARROLL, Joseph Cephas: *Slave Insurrections in the United States, 1800–1865* (Boston, Chapman & Grimes, 1938; new edn New York, New American Library, 1969).

CENTRE OF AFRICAN STUDIES, *The Transatlantic Slave Trade from West Africa* (mimeographed, Edinburgh University, 1965).

CHANNU, Pierre: *L'expansion européenne du xiiie au xve siècle* (Paris, 1969).

CHECKLAND, S.G.: "American versus West Indian Traders in Liverpool, 1793–1815", *Journal of Economic History*, 18 (1958), 141–60.

——: "Finance for the West Indies, 1780-1815", *Economic History Review*, 10 (1958), 461–9.

CHILVER, E.M. and KABERRY, P.M.: "Sources of the Nineteenth-Century Slave Trade: Two Comments", *Journal of African History*, 6 (1965), 117–20.

CHURCHILL, A. and J.: *A Collection of Voyages and Travels* (6 vols; 1732).

CLARENCE-SMITH, W.G.: "Slavery in Coastal Southern Angola, 1875–1913", *Journal of Southern African Studies*, 2, 2:14-23.

CLARKSON, Thomas: *An Essay on the Slavery and Commerce of the Human Species* (London, 1786).

——: *The History of the Rise, Progress and Accomplishment of the Abolition of the African Slave-Trade by the British Parliament* (2 vols; London, Longman, Hurst, Rees & Orme, 1808).

COHEN, David W., and GREEN, Jack P. (eds): *Neither Slave nor Free: The Freedmen of African Descent in the Slave Societies of the New World* (Baltimore, John Hopkins University Press, 1972).

COHEN, Ronald: "Slavery in Africa", *Trans-action*, 4 (1967), 44-56.

CONRAD, Alfred H., and MEYER, John R.: *The Economics of Slavery and Other Studies in Economic History* (Chicago, Aldine Publishing Co., 1964).

CONRAD, Robert: *The Destruction of Brazilian Slavery, 1850–1888* (Berkeley, University of California Press, 1972).

COOPER, F.: *Plantation Society on the East African Coast* (New Haven, Yale University Press, 1977).

——: "Studying Slavery in Africa: Some Criticisms and Comparisons", *Journal of African History*, 20 (1979), 103–25.

COQUERY, Catherine: "De la traite des esclaves a l'exportation de l'huile de palme et des palmistes au Dahomey: XIXe siècle", in Meillassoux, *Development of Indigenous Trade* (1971), 107–23.

CORWIN, Arthur F.: *Spain and the Abolition of Slavery in Cuba 1817–1886* (Austin, University of Texas, 1967).

COUPLAND, Reginald: *The British Anti-Slavery Movement* (London, Frank Cass, 1935).

——: *East Africa and its Invaders* (Oxford, Oxford University Press, 1938).

——: *The Exploitation of East Africa, 1856–1890: The Slave Trade and the Scramble* (Oxford, Oxford University Press, 1939).

CRAHAN, Margaret E. and KNIGHT, Franklin W. (eds): *Africa and the Caribbean: The legacies of a link* (Baltimore, Johns Hopkins University Press, 1979).

CRATON, Michael: *Sinews of an Empire: A Short History of British Slavery* (New York, Anchor Press, 1974; London, 1974).

——, WALVIN, James, and WRIGHT, David: *Slavery, Abolition and Emancipation: Black Slaves and the British Empire* (London, Longman, 1976).

CRONE, G.R.: *The Voyages of Cadamosto and Other Documents on Western Africa in the Second Half of the Fifteenth Century* (London, 1937).

CROW, Hugh: *Memoirs of a Slave Trader* (London, Longman, Reese etc., 1830).

CUGOANO, Ottabah: *Thoughts and Sentiments on the Evil and Wicked Traffic of the Slavery and Commerce of Species* (London, 1787).

CURTIN, Philip D.: *The Image of Africa: British Ideas and Action, 1780–1850* (Madison, University of Wisconsin Press, 1965; London, Macmillan, 1965).

——: *Africa Remembered: Narratives by West Africans from the Era of the Slave Trade* (Madison, University of Wisconsin Press, 1967).

——: "Epidemiology and the Slave Trade", *Political Science Quarterly*, 83, 2 (June 1968), 190–216.

——: *The Atlantic Slave Trade: A Census* (Madison, University of Wisconsin Press, 1969).

——: *Economic Change in Precolonial Africa: Senegambia in the Era of the Slave Trade* (Madison, University of Wisconsin Press, 1975).

——, and VANSINA, Jan: "Sources of the Nineteenth-Century Atlantic Slave Trade", *Journal of African History*, 5 (1964), 185–208.

DAAKU, Kwame Y.: "The Slave Trade and African Society", in Ranger, *Emerging Themes in African History* (London, 1968).

——: *Trade and Politics on the Gold Coast, 1600–1720* (Oxford, Clarendon Press, 1970).

——: "Trade and Trading Patterns of the Akan in the Seventeenth and Eighteenth Centuries", in Meillassoux, *Development of Indigenous Trade* (1971), 168–81.

DAGET, Serge: "L'abolition de la traite des noirs en France de 1814 à 1831", *Cahiers d'Études Africaines*, 11 (1971), 14–58.

——: "British Repression of the Illegal French Slave Trade: Some Considerations", in Gemery and Hogendorn, *Uncommon Market* (1979), 419–42.

DALBY, David: "Ashanti Survivals in the Language and Traditions of the Windward Maroons of Jamaica", *African Language Studies*, 12 (1971), 31–51.

DALLAS, R.C.: *The History of the Maroons* (London, T.N. Longman and O. Rees, 1803).

DAVIDSON, Basil: *Black Mother: Africa and the Atlantic Slave Trade* (London, 1961; revised edn Harmondsworth, Penguin, 1980).

——: *History of West Africa 1000–1800* (London, Longman, revised edn 1977).

DAVIES, K.G.: *The Royal African Company* (London, Longman, 1957).

DAVIS, David Brion: *The Problem of Slavery in Western Culture* (Ithaca,

Cornell University Press, 1966).

——: *The Problem of Slavery in the Age of Revolution, 1770–1823* (Ithaca, Cornell University Press, 1975).

DAVIS, Ralph: *The Rise of the Atlantic Economies* (Ithaca, Cornell University Press, 1973).

DEANE, Phyllis, and COLE, W.A.: *British Economic Growth, 1688–1959: Trends and Structure* (Cambridge, Cambridge University Press, 1967).

DEBBASCH, Y.: "Poésie et traite: L'opinion française sur le commerce négrier au début du XIXe siècle", *Revue Française d'Histoire d'Outre-Mer*, 48 (1961), 311–52.

DEBRUNNER, Hans W.: *Presence and Prestige: Africans in Europe* (Basler Afrika Bibliographien, Basel, 1979).

DEERR, Noel: *The History of Sugar* (2 vols; London, Chapman and Hall, 1949–50).

DEGLER, Carl N.: *Neither Black nor White: Slavery and Race Relations in Brazil and the United States* (New York, Macmillan, 1971).

DERRICK, Jonathan: *Africa's Slaves Today* (London, Allen and Unwin, 1975).

DE SOUZA, N.F: "Contribution à l'histoire de la famille Souza", *Études Dahoméenes*, 13 (1955), 17-21.

DICKSON, William: *Letters on Slavery* (London, 1789).

"DICKY SAM", A Genuine: *Liverpool and Slavery: An Historical Account of the Liverpool–African Slave Trade. Was it the cause of the Prosperity of the Town?* (Liverpool, A. Bowker & Son, 1884).

DIKE, K. Onwuka: *Trade and Politics in the Niger Delta, 1830–1885: An introduction to the economic and political history of Nigeria* (Oxford, Clarendon Press, 1956).

DONNAN, Elizabeth: *Documents Illustrative of the History of the Slave Trade to America* (4 vols; Washington, DC, Carnegie Institute, 1930–5).

DOW, George Francis: *Slave Ships and Slaving* (Salem, Maritime Research Society, 1927).

DRESCHER, Seymour: *Econocide: British Slavery in the Era of Abolition* (Pittsburgh, University of Pittsburgh Press, 1977).

DU BOIS, W.E.B.: *The Suppression of the African Slave-Trade to the United States of America, 1638–1870* (Cambridge, Harvard University Press, 1896; New York, Russell & Russell, 1965).

——: (ed.): *The Negro American Family* (Atlanta, Atlanta University Press, 1908).

DUIGNAN, Peter, and CLENDENEN, Clarence: *The United States and the African Slave Trade, 1619–1862* (Stanford, Hoover Institute, 1963).

DUMBELL, Stanley: "The Profits of the Guinea Trade", *Economic History*, 2 (1931), 254–7.

DUNN, Richard S.: *Sugar and Slaves* (Chapel Hill, University of North Carolina Press, 1972; London, Cape, 1973).

EANNES DE AZURARA, Gomes: *The Chronicle of the Discovery and Conquest of Guinea* (ed. Charles Raymond Beazely, 2 vols; New York, B. Franklin, 1937; London, Hakluyt Society, 1896–9).

EDWARDS, Bryan: *The History, Civil and Commercial, of the British Colonies in the West Indies* (3 vols; London, John Stockdale, 1801).

ELKINS, Stanley M: *Slavery: A Problem in American Institutional and Intellectual Life* (Chicago, University of Chicago Press, 1959; new edn 1963).

ELLIOTT, J.H.: *Imperial Spain 1470–1716* (New York, 1963).

ELTIS, David: "The British Transatlantic Slave Trade after 1807", *Maritime History*, 4 (1970), 1–11.

——: "The Export of Slaves from Africa, 1821–1843", *Journal of Economic History*, 37 (1977), 409–33.

——: "The British Contribution to the Nineteenth-Century Trans-Atlantic Slave Trade", *Economic History Review*, 32 (1979), 211–27.

——: "Free and Coerced Transatlantic Migrations: Some Comparisons", *American Historical Review*, 88 (1983), 251–80.

——: "The Trans-Atlantic Slave Trade, 1821–1843" (unpublished Ph.D thesis, University of Rochester, 1978).

——, and WALVIN, James (eds): *The Abolition of the Atlantic Slave Trade: Origins and Effects in Europe, Africa and the Americas* (Madison, University of Wisconsin Press, 1981).

EMMER, Pieter C.: "The History of the Dutch Slave Trade: A Bibliographical Survey", *Journal of Economic History*, XXXII, 3 (1972).

ENGERMAN, Stanley L.: "The Slave Trade and British Capital Formation of the Eighteenth Century: A Commentary on the Williams Thesis", *Business History Review*, XLVI (1972), 430–43.

——, and GENOVESE, Eugene D. (eds): *Race and Slavery in the Western Hemisphere: Quantitative Studies* (Princeton, Princeton University Press, 1975).

EQUIANO, Olaudah: *Interesting Narrative of the Life of Olaudah Equiano, or Gustavus Vassa, the African, written by himself* (London, 1789; ed. Paul Edwards, Heinemann, 1967).

FAGE, John D.: "Slavery and the Slave Trade in the Context of West African History", *Journal of African History*, 10 (1969), 393–404.

——: *A History of Africa* (London, Hutchinson, 1978).

——: "Slaves and Society in Western Africa, c. 1445–c. 1700", *Journal of African Studies*, 21 (1980), 289–310.

FALCONBRIDGE, Alexander: *An Account of the Slave Trade on the Coast of Africa* (London, 1788).

FARNIE, D.A.: "The Commercial Empire of the Atlantic, 1607–1783", *Economic History Review*, 15 (1962), 205–18.

FERNANDES, Florestan: *The Negro in Brazilian Society* (trans. Jacqueline D. Skiles, A. Brunel, Arthur Rothwell, New York, Atheneum, 1971).

FILLIOT, J.M.: *La traite des esclaves vers les Mascareignes au XVIIIe siècle* (Paris, 1974).

FISHER, Allan G.B., and FISHER, Humphrey J,: *Slavery and Muslim Society in Africa* (London, Hurst, 1970; New York, Doubleday, 1971).

FITZGERALD, Walter: *Africa: A Social, Economic and Political Geography of its Major Regions* (London, Methuen, 1967; New York, Dutton, 1957, 8th edn revised by W.C. Brice).

FLETCHER, F.T.H.: *Montesquieu and English Politics, 1750–1800* (London, E. Arnold, 1939).

FOGEL, Robert William, and ENGERMAN, Stanley L.: *Time on the Cross: The Economics of American Negro Slavery* (2 vols; Boston, Little, Brown, 1974).

FORBES, F.E.: *Dahomey and the Dahomans* (London, 1851).

FORDE, Cyril Daryll (ed.): *African Worlds* (London, Oxford University Press, 1954).

——: (ed.): *Efik Traders of Old Calabar* (London, Dawson, 1956).

——, and KABERRY, Phyllis M. (eds): *West African Kingdoms in the Nineteenth Century* (London, Oxford University Press, 1967).

FORTES, M., and EVANS-PRITCHARD, E.E. (eds): *African Political Systems* (London, Oxford University Press, 1940).

FOSTER, Charles I.: "The Colonization of Free Negroes in Liberia, 1816–35", *Journal of Negro History*, 38 (1953), 41-66.

FRAGINALS, Manuel Moreno: *El Ingenio: Complejo Económico Social Cubano del Azucar* (3 vols; Havana, 1978).

——, KLEIN, Herbert S., and ENGERMAN, Stanley L.: "The Level and Structure of Slave Prices on Cuban Plantations in the Mid-Nineteenth Century: Some Comparative Perspectives", *American Historical Review*, 88 (1983), 1201–18.

FRANKLIN, John Hope: *From Slavery to Freedom: A History of American Negroes* (Knopf, New York, 1947; 4th edn 1974).

FRAZIER, E. Franklin: *The Negro Family in the United States* (Chicago, University of Chicago Press, 1939).

——: *The Negro in the United States* (New York, Macmillan, 1949).

FREDERICKSON, George M.: *The Black Image in White Minds: The Debate on Afro-American Character and Destiny, 1817–1914* (New York, 1971).

FYFE, Christopher: "A Brief Note on the Demographic Effects of the Transatlantic Slave Trade on West Africa", *African Historical Demogra-*

phy, Centre of African Studies, Edinburgh University (Edinburgh, 1977).

FYNN, J.K.: *Asante and its Neighbours, 1700–1807* (London, Longman, 1971).

GEMERY, Henry A., and HOGENDORN, Jan S. (eds): *The Uncommon Market: Essays in the Economic History of the Atlantic Slave Trade* (New York, Academic Press, 1979).

GENOVESE, Eugene D.: *Roll, Jordan, Roll: The World the Slaves Made* (New York, Pantheon, 1972).

GOODY, Jack: "Slavery in Time and Space", in Watson, *Asian and African Systems of Slavery* (1980), 16–42.

GOVEIA, Elsa: *The West Indian Slave Laws of the 18th Century* (Caribbean Universities Press, 1970).

GRACE, John: *Domestic Slavery in West Africa* (New York, Barnes and Noble, 1975).

GRAHAM, James D.: "The Slave Trade, Depopulation and Human Sacrifice in Benin History", *Cahiers d'Études Africaines*, 5 (1965), 317–34.

GRANT, Douglas: *The Fortunate Slave: An Illustration of African Slavery in the Early Eighteenth Century* (London, Oxford University Press, 1968).

GREEN-PEDERSON, Svend E.: "The Scope and Structure of the Danish Slave Trade", *Scandinavian Economic History Review*, XIX, 2 (1971), 149–97.

GUTKIND, Peter C.W., and WALLERSTEIN, Immanuel (eds): "Africa in the Capitalist World", *Issue*, 3 (1973), 1–11.

——, and WALLERSTEIN, I. (eds): "The Three Stages of African Involvement in the World Economy", in *The Political Economy of Contemporary Africa* (Beverly Hills, Sage, 1976).

GUTMAN, Herbert G.: *The Black Family in Slavery and Freedom, 1750–1925* (New York, Pantheon, 1976).

HAIR, P.E.H.: "The Enslavement of Koelle's Informants", *Journal of African History*, 6 (1965), 193–203.

HALEY, Alex: *Roots* (New York, 1977; London, Hutchinson, 1977).

HALL, Gwendolyn: *Social Control in Slave Plantation Societies: A comparison of St Domingue and Cuba* (Baltimore, Johns Hopkins University Press, 1971).

HANCE, William A.: *The Geography of Modern Africa* (New York, Columbia University Press, 1941).

HANKE, L.: *The Spanish Struggle for Justice in the Conquest of Latin America* (Philadelphia, University of Pennsylvannia Press, 1949).

HARGREAVES, John: *Prelude to the Partition of West Africa* (London, Macmillan, 1963).

HARMS, Robert W.: "Slave Systems in Africa", *History in Africa*, 5 (1978), 327–35.

——: *River of Wealth, River of Sorrow: The Central Zaïre Basin in the Era of the Slave and Ivory Trade, 1500–1891* (New Haven, Yale University Press, 1981).

HARRIS, Joseph E. (ed.): *Global Dimensions of the African Diaspora* (Washington, DC, Howard University Press, 1982).

HARRIS, Marvin: *Patterns of Race in the Americas* (New York, Norton, 1964).

HARRIS, W.T., and SAWYER, H.: *The Springs of Mende Belief and Conduct* (Freetown, 1969).

——: *Concepts of God in Africa* (London, 1970).

HAWKINS, Joseph: *History of a Voyage to the Coast of Africa and Travels into the Interior of That Country* (Troy, 1797).

HERSKOVITS, Melville J.: *The Myth of the Negro Past* (Boston, Beacon, 1941, 1958).

HIGMAN, B.W.: *Slave Population and Economy in Jamaica, 1807–1834* (Cambridge, Cambridge University Press, 1976).

HOCHSTETTER, Franz: *Die wirtschaftlichen und politischen Motive für die Abschaffung des britischen Sklavenhandels in Jahre 1806–1807* (Leipzig, 1905).

HOETINK, H.: *Slavery and Race Relations in the Americas* (New York, 1973).

HOGG, Peter C.: *The African Slave Trade and its Suppression: A classified and Annotated Bibliography of Books, Pamphlets and Periodical Articles* (London, Frank Cass, 1973).

HOPKINS, A.G.: "Economic Imperialism in West Africa: Lagos, 1880–92", *Economic History Review*, 21 (1968), 580–606.

——: *An Economic History of West Africa* (London, Longman, 1973).

HOWARD, Warren S.: *American Slaves and the Federal Law, 1837–1862* (Berkeley, University of California Press, 1963).

HYDE, F.E., PARKINSON, B.B., and MARRINER, S.: "The Nature and Profitability of the Liverpool Slave Trade", *Economic History Review*, 5 (1953) 368–77.

INIKORI, J.E.: "Measuring the Atlantic Slave Trade: An Assessment of Curtin and Anstey", *Journal of African History*, 17 (1976), 197–223.

——: "The Import of Firearms into West Africa, 1750–1807: A Quantitative Analysis", *Journal of African History*, 18 (1977), 339–68.

——: "The Origin of the Diaspora: The Slave Trade from Africa", *Tarikh*, 5 (1978), 1–19.

——: *Forced Migration: The Impact of the Export Slave Trade on African Societies* (London, Hutchinson, 1982).

INNES, C.M.: *England and Slavery* (London, 1934).

IRWIN, Graham W.: *Africans Abroad: A documentary history of the black diaspora in Asia, Latin America and the Caribbean during the age of slavery* (New York, Columbia University Press, 1977).

ISERT, Paul Erdmann: *Reise nach Guinea and den Caribaischen Insel in Columbian* (Copenhagen, 1788).

JAKOBSSON, Stiv: *Am I not a Man and a Brother* (Uppsala, 1972).

JAMES, C.L.R.: *The Black Jacobins: Toussaint L'Ouverture and the San Domingo Revolution* (London, 1938, Allison and Busby, 1980; Vintage Books, New York, 1963).

JOBSON, Richard: *The Golden Trade: or, A discovery of the River Gambia, and the Golden Trade of the Aethiopians* (London, Nicholas Bourne, 1623).

JOHNSON, Marion: "The Ounce in Eighteenth-Century West African Trade", *Journal of African History*, 7 (1966), 197–214.

——: "The Atlantic Slave Trade and the Economy of West Africa", in Anstey and Hair, *Liverpool, The African Slave Trade*, vol. 2 (1976) 14–38.

——: "Census, Map and Guesstimate: The Past Population of the Accra Region", in *African Historical Demography*, Centre of African Studies, Edinburgh University, 272–93.

JONES, G.I.: *The Trading States of the Oil Rivers* (London, Oxford University Press, 1963).

JORDAN, Winthrop D.: *White over Black: American Attitudes Towards the Negro, 1550–1812* (Chapel Hill, University of North Carolina Press, 1968).

KAY, George: *The Shameful Trade* (London, Muller, 1967).

KILSON, Martin L., and ROTBERG, Robert I. (eds): *The African Diaspora: Interpretive Essays* (Cambridge, Mass., Harvard University Press, 1978).

KLEIN, Herbert S.: *Slavery in the Americas: A Comparative Study of Virginia and Cuba* (Chicago, University of Chicago Press, 1967).

——: "Slave Mortality on British Ships, 1791–1797", in Anstey and Hair, *Liverpool* (1976).

——: *The Middle Passage: Comparative Studies in the Atlantic Slave Trade* (Princeton, Princeton University Press, 1978).

——, and ENGERMAN, Stanley L. (eds): "Facteures de mortalité dans le trafic français d'esclaves au xviii siècle", *Annales, Économies, Sociétés, Civilisations*, xxxi, 6 (1976), 1213–24.

——, and ENGERMAN, Stanley L. (eds): "A Note on Mortality in the French Slave Trade in the Eighteenth Century", in Gemery and Hogendorn, *Uncommon Market* (1979), 261–72.

KLEIN, Martin A.: "Slavery, the Slave Trade and Legitimate Commerce in Late Nineteenth-Century Africa", *Études d'Histoire Africaine*, 2 (1971), 5–28.

——: "Shipping Patterns and Mortality in the African Slave Trade to Rio de Janeiro, 1825–1830", *Cahiers d'Études Africaines*, XV, 55 (1975), 381–98.

——: "The Study of Slavery in Africa: A Review Article", *Journal of African History*, 19 (1978), 599–609.

KLINGBERG, Frank J.: *The Anti-Slavery Movement in England* (New Haven, Yale University Press, 1926).

KNIGHT, Franklin W.: *Slave Society in Cuba during the Nineteenth Century* (Madison, University of Wisconsin Press, 1970).

LABARTHE, P.: *Voyage au Sénégal pendant les années 1784 et 1785* (Paris, 1802).

LABAT, Jean Baptiste: *Nouveau voyage aux isles de L'Amérique* (Paris, 1722).

LA FARGE, John: *Race Questions and the Negro* (New York, 1945).

LATHAM, A.J.H.: "Currency, Credit and Capitalism on the Cross River in the Pre-Colonial Era", *Journal of African History*, 12 (1971), 599–605.

——: *Old Calabar, 1600–1891: The Impact of the International Economy upon a Traditional Society* (Oxford, Oxford University Press, 1973).

LAW, R.C.C.: "Royal Monopoly and Private Enterprise in the Atlantic Trade; The Case of Dahomey", *Journal of African History*, 18 (1977), 555–77.

——: "Slaves, Trade and Taxes: The Material Basis of Political Power in Pre-Colonial West Africa", *Research in Economic Anthropology*, 1, 37–52.

LAW, Robin: *The Oyo Empire c.1600–c.1836* (Oxford, Clarendon Press, 1977).

LENZINGER, Elsy: *The Art of Black Africa* (New York, 1972).

LEVEEN, E. Phillip: "The African Slave Supply Response", *African Studies Review*, 18 (1975), 9–28.

——: *British Slave Trade Suppression Policies, 1821–1865* (Arno Press, New York, 1977).

LLOYD, Christopher: *The Navy and the Slave Trade: The Suppression of the African Slave in the Nineteenth Century* (London, Longman, 1949).

LOVEJOY, Paul E.: *The Ideology of Slavery in Africa* (Beverly Hills, 1981).

——: "The Volume of the Atlantic Slave Trade: A Synthesis", *Journal of African Studies*, 22 (1982).

——: *Transformations in Slavery* (Cambridge, Cambridge University Press, 1983).

LUTTERELL, Anthony: "Slavery and Slaving in the Portuguese Atlantic (to about 1500)", in Fyfe, *Transatlantic Slave Trade* (1965).

LY, Abdoulaye: *La Compagnie du Sénégal* (Paris, 1958).

MACINNES, C.M.: *England and Slavery* (Bristol, Arrowsmith, 1934).

——: "The Slave Trade", in Parkinson, *Trade Winds* (1948).

MACKENZIE-GRIEVE, Averil: *The Last Years of the English Slave Trade, Liverpool, 1750–1807* (London, Putnam, 1941).

MAGALHAES-GODINHO, Vitorino: *L'économie de l'empire portugais aux xve et xvie siècles* (Paris, 1969).

MANNING, Patrick: "Slaves, Palm Oil and Political Power on the West African Coast", *African Historical Studies*, 2 (1969), 279–88.

——: "The Slave Trade in Southern Dahomey", in Gemery and Hogendorn, *Uncommon Market* (1979), 107–41.

——: "The Enslavement of Africans: A Demographic Model", *Canadian Journal of African Studies*, 15, 3, 499–526.

——: *Slavery, Colonialism and Economic Growth in Dahomey, 1640–1960* (Cambridge, Cambridge University Press, 1982).

——: "Growth Despite Slavery and Taxes: The Bight of Benin, 1640–1960", paper presented to African Studies Association meeting (Baltimore, 1978).

——: "Contours of Slavery and Social Change in Africa", *American Historical Review*, 88, 4 (1983), 835–57.

MANNIX, Daniel P., and COWLEY, Malcolm: *Black Cargoes: A History of the Atlantic Slave Trade. 1518–1865* (New York, Viking Press, 1962; London, Longman, 1963).

MARSHALL, Peter: *The Anti-Slave Trade Movement in Bristol* (Bristol, 1968).

MARTIN, Gaston: *Nantes au XVIIIe siècle: L'ère de négriers, 1714–44* (Paris, 1931).

——: *Histoire de l'Esclavage dans les Colonies Françaises* (Paris, 1948).

MARTIN, Phyllis M.: *The External Trade of the Loango Coast, 1576–1870* (Oxford, Clarendon Press, 1972).

MASON, Michael: "Population Density and 'Slave Raiding': the Case of the Middle Belt of Nigeria", *Journal of African History*, 10 (1969), 551–64.

MATHEWS, DONALD G.: *Slavery and Methodism: A chapter in American morality, 1780–1845* (Princeton, Princeton University Press, 1965).

MATHIESON, William Law: *British Slavery and its Abolition, 1823–1838* (London, 1926).

——: *Great Britain and the Slave Trade, 1839–1865* (New York, Octagon Books, 1929).

MATTHEWS, John: *A Voyage to the River Sierra Leone on the Coast of Africa* (London, 1788).

MAURO, Frederic: *Étude économique sur l'expansion portugaise, 1500–1900* (Paris, 1970).

——: *Portugal et l'Atlantic au xviie siècle: étude économique* (Paris, 1970).

MEILLASSOUX, Claude (ed.): *The Development of Indigenous Trade and*

Markets in West Africa (Oxford, 1971).

——: (ed.): *L'esclavage en Afrique pré-coloniale* (Paris, Maspero, 1975).

MELLAFE, Rolando: *Negro Slavery in Latin America* (Berkeley, University of California Press, 1971).

MELLOR, G.R.: *British Imperial Trusteeship, 1783–1850* (London, Faber and Faber, 1951).

MERRITT, J.E.: "The Liverpool Slave Trade from 1789 to 1791" (University of Nottingham M.A. thesis, 1959).

——: "The Triangular Trade", *Business History*, 3 (1960), 1–7.

METTAS, Jean: "Honfleur et la traite des noirs au XVIIIᵉ siècle", *Revue Française d'Histoire d'Outre-Mer*, LX (1973), 5–26.

——: "La traite portugaise en haute Guinée 1758–1797: problèmes et méthodes", *Journal of African History*, 16 (1975), 342–63.

——: "Pour une histoire de la traite des noirs français: sources et problèmes", *Revue Française d'Histoire d'Outre-Mer*, LXII (1975), 19–46.

——: *Répertoire des expeditions négrières française au XVIIIᵉ siècle* (ed. Serge Daget; Nantes, 1978).

MEYER, Jean: "Le commerce négrier nantais, 1774–1792", *Annales*, 15 (1960), 120–9.

——: *L'Armement Nantais dans la deuxième moitié du XVIII siècle* (Paris, 1969).

MIDDLETON, John, and TAIT, David (eds): *Tribes without Rulers* (London, Oxford University Press,1958).

MIERS, Suzanne: *Britain and the Ending of the Slave Trade* (London, Longman, 1975).

MIERS, S., and KOPYTOFF, I. (eds): *Slavery in Africa: Historical and Anthropological Perspectives* (Madison, University of Wisconsin Press, 1977).

MILLER, Joseph C.: "Legal Portuguese Slaving from Angola: Some Preliminary Indications of Volume and Direction, 1760–1830", in Minchinton and Emmer, *Atlantic Slave Trade* (1976), 135–71; *Revue Française d'Histoire d'Outre-Mer*, lx, 226–7 (1975), 135–76.

——: *Slavery: A Comparative Teaching Bibliography* (Waltham, 1877).

——: "The Slave Trade in Congo and Angola", in Kilson and Rotberg, *African Diaspora* (1978), 75–113.

——: "Mortality in the Atlantic Slave Trade: Statistical Evidence on Causality", *Journal of Interdisciplinary History*, xi, 3 (1981), 385–423.

MINCHINTON, Walter E.: *The Trade of Bristol in the Eighteenth Century*, (Bristol, 1966).

——, and EMMER, Pieter C. (eds): *The Atlantic Slave Trade, New Approaches* (Paris, 1975).

MINTZ, Sidney W. (ed.): *Slavery, Colonialism and Racism* (New York, Norton, 1974).

——, and PRICE, Richard (eds): *An Anthropological Approach to the Afro-American Past: A Caribbean Perspective* (Philadelphia, 1976).

MITCHELL, B.R., and DEANE, Phyllis: *Abstract of British Historical Statistics* (Cambridge, Cambridge University Press, 1962).

MOORE, Francis: *Travels into the Inland Parts of Africa* (London, 1738).

MÖRNER, Magnus: *Race Mixture in the History of Latin America* (Boston, 1967).

MORTON WILLIAMS, Peter: "The Oyo Yoruba and the Atlantic Trade, 1690–1830", *Journal of the Historical Society of Nigeria*, 3 (1964), 25–45.

MOSS, R.P., and RATHBONE, R.J.A.: *The Population Factor in African Society* (London, University of London Press, 1975).

MURDOCK, George Peter: *Africa: Its People and their Cultural History* (New York, 1959).

MURRAY, David R.: "Statistics of the Slave Trade to Cuba, 1790–1867", *Journal of Latin American Studies*, 3 (1971), 131–49.

——: *Odious Commerce: Britain, Spain and the Abolition of the Cuban Slave Trade* (Cambridge, Cambridge University Press, 1980).

NEWBURY, C.W.: *The Western Slave Coast and its Rulers* (Oxford, Clarendon Press, 1961).

NEWTON, John: *An Authentic Narrative of Some Remarkable and Interesting Paticulars in the Life of John Newton Communicated in a Series of Letters to the Reverend Mr Haweis* (London, 1782).

——: *Letters to a Wife* (London, 1793).

——: *The Journal of a Slave Trader 1750–1754* (ed. Bernard Martin and Mark Spurrell; London, Epworth Press, 1962).

NIEBOER, H.J.: *Slavery as an Industrial System: Ethnological Researches* (The Hague, 1900).

NKETIA, J.H. Kwabena: *The Music of Africa* (New York, Norton, 1974; London, Gollancz, 1975).

NORREGARD, George: *Danish Settlements in West Africa 1658–1850* (trans. Sigurd Mammen; Boston, Boston University Press, 1966).

NORRIS, Robert: *Memoirs of the Reign of Bossa Ahadee, King of Dahomey* (London, 1789).

NORTHRUP, David: *Trade without Rulers: Pre-Colonial Economic Development in South-Eastern Nigeria* (Oxford, Clarendon Press, 1978).

NWULIA, Moses D.W.: *Britain and Slavery in East Africa* (Washington, DC, Three Continents Press, 1975).

OBICHERE, Boniface: "Women and Slavery in the Kingdom of Dahomey", *Revue Française d'Histoire d'Outre-Mer*, 65 (1978), 5–20.

OGEDEMGBE, K.O.: "The Kingdom of the Lower Nile, c.1650–1900" (unpublished Ph.D thesis, University of Wisconsin, 1971).

OPOKU, Kofi Asare: *West African Traditional Religion* (Accra, 1978).

OWEN, Nicholas: *Journal of a Slave-Dealer, 1754–1759* (ed. Eveline C. Martin: London, 1930).

PALMER, Colin: *Human Cargoes: The British Slave Trade to Spanish America, 1700–1739* (Urbana, University of Illinois Press, 1981).

PARES, Richard: "The Economic Factors in the History of the Empire", *Economic History Review*, VII (1936–7), 119–37.

——: *A West Indian Fortune* (Hamden, Archon Books, 1956; London, Longman, 1956).

PARKINSON, C. Northcote (ed.): *The Trade Winds: A Study of British Overseas Trade during the French Wars 1793–1815* (London, Allen & Unwin, 1948).

—: *The Rise of the Port of Liverpool* (Liverpool, 1952).

PARRINDER, E.G.: *West African Religion* (London, Epworth Press, 1961).

PARRY, J.H. and SHERLOCK, P.M.: *A Short History of the West Indies* (London, Macmillan, 1963).

PATTERSON, Orlando: *The Sociology of Slavery: An Analysis of the Origins, Development and Structure of Negro Slave Society in Jamaica* (London, Macgibbon & Kee, 1967).

——: *Slavery and Social Death: A comparative study* (Cambridge, Mass., Harvard University Press, 1982).

PESCATELLO, Ann M. (ed.): *The African in Latin America* (New York, Knopf, 1975).

PEUKERT, Werner: *Der Atlantische Sklavenhandel von Dahomey, 1740–1779. Wirtschaftsanthropologie und Sozialgeschichte* (Wiesbaden, 1978).

PHILLIPS, Ulrich Bonnell: *American Negro Slavery: A Survey of the Supply, Employment and Control of Negro Labour as Determined by the Plantation Regime* (New York, 1918: Baton Rouge, Louisiana State University Press, 1966).

PITMAN, Frank Wesley: *The Development of the British West Indies, 1700–1763* (Yale Historical Publications Studies, IV, New Haven, Yale University Press, 1917; Hamden, Archon Books, 1967).

POKU, K.: "Traditional Roles and People of Slave Origin in Modern Ashanti: A Few Impressions", *Ghana Journal of Sociology*, 6 (1979), 34–8.

POLANYI, Karl: *Dahomey and the Slave Trade: An Analysis of an Archaic Economy* (Seattle, University of Washington Press, 1966).

POPE-HENNESSEY, James: *Sins of the Fathers: A Study of the Atlantic Slave Traders, 1441–1807* (London, Weidenfeld, 1967; New York, Knopf, 1968).

PORTER, Dale H.: *The Abolition of the Slave Trade in England, 1784–1807* (Hamden, Archon Books, 1970).

POSTLETHWAYT, Malachy: *The African Trade, the Great Pillar and Support of the British Plantation Trade in America* (London, J. Robinson, 1745).

——: *The National and Private Advantage of the Africa Trade Considered...* (London, John and Paul Knapton, 1746).

——: *Considerations On the Revival of the Royal-British-Assiento; between His Catholick Majesty, And the Honourable The South-Sea Company* (London, John and Paul Knapton, 1749).

——: *The Importance of the Africa Expedition Considered* (London, M. Cooper, 1758).

POSTMA, Johannes: "The Dimension of the Dutch Slave Trade from Western Africa", *Journal of African History*, 13 (1972), 237–48.

——: "The Origin of African Slaves: The Dutch Activities of the Guinea Coast, 1675–1795", in Engerman and Genovese, *Race and Slavery* (1975).

——: "The Dutch Slave Trade: A Quantitative Assessment", in Minchinton and Emmer, *Atlantic Slave Trade* (1975), 232–44.

——: "Mortality in the Dutch Slave Trade, 1675–1795", in Gemery and Hogendorn, *Uncommon Market* (1979), 239–65.

PRICE, Richard (ed.): *Maroon Societies: Rebel Slave Communities in the Americas* (New York, Doubleday Anchor, 1973).

PRIESTLEY, Margaret: *West African Trade and Coast Society: A Family Study* (London, Oxford University Press, 1969).

RABOTEAU, Albert J.: *Slave Religion* (New York, Oxford University Press, 1978).

RAGATZ, L.J.: *The Fall of the Planter Class in the British Caribbean, 1763–1833* (London, 1928).

RANGER, Terence (ed.): *Emerging Themes of African History* (London, Heinmann, 1968).

RANSFORD, Oliver: *The Slave Trade: The Story of Transatlantic Slavery* (London, J. Murray, 1971).

RATTRAY, R.S.: *Ashanti Law and Constitution* Oxford, Clarendon Press, 1929).

RAWLEY, James A.: "The Port of London and the Eighteenth Century Slave Trade: Historians, Sources and a Reappraisal", *African Economic History*, 9 (1980), 85–100.

——: *The Transatlantic Slave Trade: A History* (New York, Norton, 1981).

REEFE, Thomas Q.: *The Rainbow and the Kings: A History of the Luba Empire to 1891* (Berkeley, University of California Press, 1981).

REYNOLDS, Edward: "Agricultural Adjustments on the Gold Coast After the End of the Slave Trade, 1807–1874", *Agricultural History*, 47 (1973), 308–18.

——: *Trade and Economic Change on the Gold Coast, 1807–1874* (London, Longman, 1974).

RICE, C. Duncan: *The Rise and Fall of Black Slavery* (London, Macmillan, 1975; New York, Harper & Row, 1975).

RICHARDSON, David P.: "The Bristol Slave Trade in the Eighteenth Century" (University of Manchester M.A. thesis, 1969).

——: "Profitability in the Bristol-Liverpool Slave Trade", in Minchinton and Emmer, *Atlantic Slave Trade* (1975), 301–8; *Revue Française d'Histoire d'Outre-Mer*, LXII (1975), 226–7.

——: "Profits in the Eighteenth-Century British Slave Trade: The Accounts of William Davenport of Liverpool", in Anstey and Hair, *Liverpool* (1976), 60–90.

RICHARDSON, Patrick: *Empire and Slavery* (London, Longman, 1968).

RODNEY, Walter: "African Slavery and Other Forms of Social Oppression on the Upper Guinea Coast, in the Context of the Atlantic Slave-Trade", *Journal of African History*, 7, 3 (1966), 431–43.

——: *West Africa and the Atlantic Slave Trade* (Nairobi, Historical Association of Tanzania, Paper No.2, 1967).

——: "Gold and Slaves on the Gold Coast", *Transactions of the Historical Society of Ghana*, 10 (1969), 13–2.

——: "Upper Guinea and the Significance of the Origins of Africans Enslaved in the New World", *Journal of Negro History*, 54 (1969), 327–45.

——: *A History of the Upper Guinea Coast, 1545–1800* (Oxford, Clarendon Press, 1970).

——: *How Europe Underdeveloped Africa* (London, Bogle-L'Ouverture Publications, 1972; Washington, DC, Howard University Press, 1974).

ROMER, Ludewig Ferdinand: *Tilforladelig Efterrentning om Kysten Guinea* (Copenhagen, 1760).

RONEN, Dov: "On the African Role in the Trans-Atlantic Slave Trade in Dahomey", *Cahiers d'Études Africaines*, 11 (1971), 5–13.

ROSENBLAT, Angel: *La Población Indígena y el Mestizaje en America* (2 vols, Buenos Aires, 1954).

ROSS, David A.: "The Career of Domingo Martinez in the Bight of Benin, 1833–64", *Journal of African History*, 6 (1965), 79–90.

ROUT, Leslie B., JR.: *The African Experience in Spanish America: 1502 to the Present Day* (Cambridge, Cambridge University Press, 1976).

RUBIN, Vera, and TUDEN, Arthur (eds): "Comparative Perspectives on Slavery in New World Plantation Societies", *Annals of the New York Academy of Sciences* (New York, 1977).

RUSSELL-WOOD, A.J.R.: *The Black Man in Slavery and Freedom in Colonial Brazil* (London, 1982).

RYDER, Allan F.C.: *Benin and the Europeans, 1485–1897* (London, Longman, 1969).

SANCHEZ-ALBORNOZ, Nicolas: *The Population of Latin America: A History* (Berkeley, University of California Press, 1974).

SAUER, Carl Ortwin: *The Early Spanish Main* (Berkeley, University of California Press, 1969).

SAUNDERS, A.C. De C.M.: *A Social History of Black Slaves and Freedmen in Portugal, 1441–1555* (Cambridge, Cambridge University Press, 1982).

SAWYER, Harry: *God: Ancestor or Creator* (London, 1970).

SCHELLE, Georges: *La traite négrière aux Indes de Castille* (2 vols, Paris, 1906).

SCHWARTZ, Stuart B.: "Indian Labor and New World Plantations: European Demands and Indian Responses in Northeast Brazil", *American Historical Review*, 87 (1982), 55–86.

SEEBER, Edward Derbyshire: *Anti-Slavery Opinion in France during the Second Half of the Eighteenth Century* (Baltimore, 1937).

SHARP, Granville: *A Representation of the Injustice and Dangerous Tendancy of Tolerating Slavery or of Admitting the least claims to Private Property in the Persons of the Men of England* (London, 1769).

SHERIDAN, Richard B.: "The Commercial and Financial Organization of the British Slave Trade, 1750–1807", *Economic History Review*, 11 (December 1958), 249–63.

——: "The Wealth of Jamaica in the Eighteenth Century", *Economic History Review*, 18 (1965), 292–311.

——: "The Plantation Revolution and the Industrial Revolution, 1625–1775", *Caribbean Studies*, 9 (October 1969), 5-25.

——: *The Development of the Plantations to 1750* (Caribbean Universities Press, 1970).

——: *Sugar and Slavery: An Economic History of the British West Indies 1623–1775* (Baltimore, Johns Hopkins University Press, 1973).

SHYLLON, Folarin O.: *Black Slaves in Britain* (London, Institute of Race Relations/Oxford University Press, 1974).

——: *Black People in Britain 1555–1833* (London, Institute of Race Relations/Oxford University Press, 1977).

SIMPSON, L.B.: *The Encomienda in New Spain: The Beginning of Spanish Mexico* (Berkeley, University of California Press, 1950).

SKINNER, Elliott P. (ed.): *Peoples and Cultures of Africa* (New York, 1973).

SMITH, John David: *Black Slavery in the Americas: An Interdisciplinary Bibliography, 1865–1980* (Westport, Conn., 1982).

SMITH, Michael G.: "Slavery and Emancipation in Two Societies", *Social and Economic Studies*, 3 (1954), 239–80.

SMITH, William: *A New Voyage to Guinea* (London, 1744).

SNELGRAVE, William: *A New Account of Some Parts of Guinea, and the Slave Trade* (London, 1734).

STEIN, Robert Louis: "The Profitability of the Nantes Slave Trade", *Journal of Economic History*, 35 (1975), 779–93.

——: "Measuring the French Slave Trade, 1713–1792–3", *Journal of African History*, xix, 4 (1978).

——: *The French Slave Trade in the Eighteenth Century* (Madison, 1979).

STEIN, Stanley J.: *Vassouras, A Brazilian Coffee County, 1850–1900* (Cambridge, Mass., Harvard University Press, 1957).

SUTCH, Richard: "The Profitability of Antebellum Slavery — Revisited", *Southern Economic Journal*, XXXI (1965), 365–77.

SYPHER, Wylie: "Hutcheson and Classical Theory of Slavery", *Journal of Negro History*, XXVI (1939), 263–80.

——: *Guinea's Captive Kings: British Anti-Slavery Literature of the Eighteenth Century* (New York, 1942).

TEMPERLEY, Howard: "Anti-Slavery Ideology", in Eltis and Walvin, *Abolition of the Atlantic Trade* (1981), 21–35.

TERRAY, Emmanuel: "Long-Distance Exchange and the Formation of the State: The Case of the Abron Kingdom of Gyaman", *Economy and Society*, 3 (1974), 315–45.

——: "La captivité dans le royaume abron de Gyaman", in Meillassoux, *L'esclavage en Afrique pré-coloniale* (1975), 345–89.

——: "Contribution à une étude de l'armée asante", *Cahiers d'Études Africaines*, 16 (1976), 297–356.

THOMAS, Robert P.: "The Sugar Colonies of the Old Empire: Profit or Loss for Great Britain?", *Economic History Review*, 2nd series, 21 (1968), 30–45.

THOMPSON, V.B.: *The Making of the African Diaspora in the Americas 1441–1900* (London, Longman, 1984).

THORNTON, A.P.: "The Organization of the Slave Trade in the English West Indies, 1660–1685", *William and Mary Quarterly*, 12 (1955), 399–409.

THORNTON, John: "The Slave Trade in Eighteenth-Century Angola: Effects on Demographic Structures", *Canadian Journal of African Studies*, 14 (1980), 417–27.

TREPP, Jean: "The Liverpool Movement for the Abolition of the English Slave Trade", *Journal of Negro History*, 13 (1928), 265–85.

UCHENDU, Victor C.: *The Igbo of Southeast Nigeria* (New York, Holt, Rinehart & Winston, 1965).

——: "Slavery in Southeast Nigeria", *Trans-Action*, 4 (1967), 52–4.

UNGER, W.S.: "Bijdraen tot de geschiedenis", *Economisch Historisch Jaarboek*, 28 (1958).

UZOIGWE, G.N.: "The Slave Trade and African Societies", *Transactions of the Historical Society of Ghana*, XIV, 2 (December 1973), 187–212.

VALLADARES, Clarival Do Prado (ed.): *The Impact of African Culture on Brazil* (Rio de Janeiro, 1977).

VANSINA, Jan: *Kingdoms of the Savannah* (Madison, 1968).

——: *Art History in Africa* (London, 1984).

VERGER, Pierre: *Bahia and the West Coast Trade, 1549–1851* (Ibadan, 1964).

——: *Flux et reflux de la traite des nègres entre le golfe de Bénin et Bahia de Todos os Santos du 17ᵉ et au 19ᵉ siècle* (Paris and The Hague, 1968).

VERLINDEN, Charles: *The Beginnings of Modern Colonization: Eleven Essays* (trans. Y. Freccero; Ithaca, Cornell University Press, 1970).

VILES, Perry: "The Slaving Interest in the Atlantic Ports, 1763–1792", *French Historical Studies*, 7 (1972), 529–44.

VOGT, John L.: "The Early São Tomé-Principe Slave Trade with Mina, 1500–1540", *International Journal of African Historical Studies*, 6, 3, 453–67.

——: *Portuguese Rule on the Gold Coast, 1469–1682* (Athens, University of Georgia, 1979).

WADSTROM, Carl Bernhard: *Observations on the Slave Trade* (London, 1789).

WALKER, James W. St G.: *The Black Loyalists: The Search for a promised land in Nova Scotia and Sierra Leone, 1783–1870* (New York, Africana Publishing Co., 1976).

WALLERSTEIN, Immanuel: *The Modern World System: Capitalist Agriculture and the Origins of the European World-Economy in the Sixteenth Century* (New York, Academic Press, 1974).

WALVIN, James: *The Black Presence: A documentary history of the Negro in England, 1555–1860* (London, Orbach and Chambers, 1971).

——: *Black and White: The Negro and English Society, 1555–1945* (London, Allen Lane, 1973).

WATSON, James L. (ed.): *Asian and African Systems of Slavery* (Oxford, 1980).

WESLEY, John: *Thoughts Upon Slavery* (London, 1774).

WEST, Richard: *Back to Africa: A History of Sierra Leone and Liberia* (London, Cape, 1970).

WILBERFORCE, Robert and Samuel: *The Life of William Wilberforce* (5 vols, London, 1838).

WILBERFORCE, William: *An Appeal. . . in behalf of the Negro Slaves in the*

West Indies (London, 1823).

WILLETT, Frank: *African Art* (London, Thames & Hudson, 1970; New York, Praeger, 1971).

WILLIAMS, Eric: *Capitalism and Slavery* (Chapel Hill, University of North Carolina, 1944; London, Deutsch, 1964).

——: *From Columbus to Castro: The history of the Caribbean, 1492– 1969* (London, Deutsch, 1970).

WILLIAMS, Gomer: *History of the Liverpool Privateers and Letters of Marque with an Account of the Liverpool Slave Trade* (London, 1897).

WILLIAMS, J.J.: *Voodoos and Obeas* (London, 1964).

WOOD, Peter H.: *Black Majority* (New York, Knopf, 1964).

WRIGLEY, Christopher: "Historicism in Africa", *African Affairs*, 279, 70 (1971), 113–34.

WYLIE, Kenneth C.: "The Slave Trade in Nineteenth-Century Tenneland and the British Sphere of Influence", *African Studies Review*, 16, 2, 203–17.

WYNDHAM, Hugh A.: *The Atlantic and Slavery* (London, Oxford University Press, 1935).

——: *The Atlantic and Emancipation* (London, Oxford University Press, 1937).

Index

173